AF304738

Serena Solin

A Barer Sky

Winter Editions, 2026

Contents

A Barer Sky

Weeping Angel

The human soul is a clearing in a forest and
for the divinely pure and untarnished, it must
be hard to understand why it's forever getting
choked with growth.

Karl Ove Knausgård

when Knausgård says this
he is speaking of angels
in a way I can or will not speak of angels
having seen—

let me start again

I come alone through the courtyard
on one of spring's first full days
and encounter a woman on a laptop
and, by her side, a rabbit

I had just read about a rabbit
a world-record-holding rabbit
that had died in the carriage
of an airplane, on a voyage

I greet the woman and the rabbit
and they mutually ignore me
they are both tenants
what weapon could defend them

they snap their own necks
under stress, rabbits

it is a single weapon, it is not enough
it is online shopping in my bed for body
armor, it is not enough

back then I slid around the country
now I know that was all it was
because here are the restaurants

here are the courts, hoops deleted
here are the umbrella heaters
in anticipation of a winter

we will spend, if we are out,
outside, the city already preparing
for electrical fires, the little mortal

waves as they swell in pure relation
to nothing, countless doorways

in the yard across the way from M's house
in my sister's dream, looming by her nightstand
there are rabbits
of different sizes, of different
aliveness
(alivenesses)
oddly still, observing

still you make your own life
though it begins before you are ready
and there is never enough time
there are rabbits

even the dead one
whose skin I keep
change inside

back in the day of museums
if you remember
there was one north of the city
where a room had been styled to resemble
the simple quarters of the early Christians

on the wall of that room
a painting of precisely that room
but in that image, annunciation

tell me an angel
a trick of the eye

for this purpose
a weapon

throw your life away

what happens then
I don't demand to know

there is a high school on the beach
where the bleachers look over at the city beyond
and beyond that, ocean

even one October
mid-Monday
there is no one

a gap opens between the populous
and sparse worlds

and what appears there
is leporine

NOTES ON SELF-RELIANCE
A POEM FOR TWO VOICES

Man is his own **lonely** star; and the soul that can
Render an honest and a perfect man,
Commands all light, all influence, all fate;
Nothing to him falls early or too late.
Our acts our angels are, or good or ill,
Our fatal shadows that walk by us still,
impress upon the universal velvet.

Epilogue to Beaumont and Fletcher's
Honest Man's Fortune

Cast the bantling on the rocks,
Suckle him with the she-wolf's teat;
Wintered with the hawk and fox,
Power and speed be hands and feet.

Let the child see the rain
Scatter hydrangeas round his grave
On his stone a plastic train
Passes through his dream hallways

I.

How the Connection of Events Shatters

I read the other day **as summer sluiced through fall, days without attendant nights,** some verses written by an eminent painter which were original and not conventional. Always the soul hears **always the soul** an admonition in such lines, let the subject be what it may. The sentiment they **instill** is of more value than any thought they may contain, **too igneous to touch, exchanged for what crystallizes, what is left over.** To believe your own thought **and turn away from knowledge,** to believe that what is true for you in your private heart is true for all men **and to be terribly ashamed,**—that is genius **in its black splendor, how it stormed, a tree of crows.** Speak your latent conviction, and it shall be the universal sense; for the inmost becomes the outmost **fear**—and our first thought is rendered back to us by the trumpets of the Last Judgment. Familiar as the voice of the mind is to each, the highest merit we ascribe to Moses, Plato, and Milton **whom once we loved** is that they set at naught books and traditions, and spoke not what men, but what they thought, **the broken tower of their imagination.** A man should learn to detect **with his ear to the ground for hoofbeats** and watch that gleam of light **divining rod** which flashes across his mind from within, more than the lustre of the firmament of bards and sages **giving away** their position by fire. Yet he dismisses without notice his thought, because it is his. **Mine.** In every work of genius we recognize our own rejected thoughts; they come back to us **like mysterious lights on the road beyond the national border** with a certain alienated majesty. Great works of art have no more affecting lesson for us, **nothing else for us**, than this. They teach us to abide by our spontaneous impression with good-humored **shopkeeper's** inflexibility then most when the whole cry of voices is on the other side. Else tomorrow a stranger will say with masterly good sense precisely what we have thought and felt all the time, and we shall be forced to take with shame our own opinion from another. **She said what I knew to be true with some kindness, and with an open heart I heard it, but still I was alone, as distant from the stranger as the beloved.**

There is a time in every man's education when he arrives at the **healing** conviction that envy is ignorance; that imitation is suicide; that he must take himself for better for worse as his portion **mostly worse**; that though the wide universe is full of good, no kernel of nourishing corn can come to him but through his toil bestowed on that plot of ground which is given to him to till **which as he tills grows ever larger.** The power which resides in him is new in nature **like a church with no shadows**, and none but he knows what that is which he can do, nor does he know until he has tried **and failed.** Not for nothing one face, one character, one fact, **one spirit, pagan icon,** makes much impression on him, and another none. It is not without preestablished harmony, this sculpture in the memory **no shadows**. The eye **closed against the day** was placed where one ray should fall, that it might testify of that particular ray **a difficult anniversary**. Bravely let him speak the utmost syllable of his confession. **Words turn to ice as they leave our lips.** We but half express ourselves, and are ashamed of that divine idea **shatter** which each of us represents. It may be safely trusted as proportionate and of good issues, so it be faithfully imparted, but God will not have his work made manifest by cowards. It needs a divine man to exhibit anything divine. A man is relieved and gay **and finally sleeps** when he has put his heart into his work and done his best; but what he has said or done otherwise shall give him no peace. **Your insomnia.*** It is a deliverance which does not deliver. In the attempt his genius deserts him; no muse befriends **stands at the riverbank washing her basket of clothes**; no invention, **no intervention**, no hope.

Trust thyself: every heart vibrates to that iron string. Accept the place the divine providence has found for you, the society of your contemporaries, **how** the connection of events **shatters**. Great men have always done so, and confided **confined** themselves childlike to the genius of their age, betraying their perception that the

---

*   VIEW ONE: facing north
    the bridge that cross-binds

    the territories, the sugar factory
    at the foot, the lights.

    VIEW TWO: tiny windows
    and how they diffuse

    a mauve that afflicts
    all the facets of your vision

    continuously shifting,
    unextinguished, the lights.

Eternal was stirring **playing house** at their heart, working through their hands **I sigh at**, predominating in all their being. And we are now **all of us** men, and must accept in the highest mind the same transcendent destiny; and not pinched in a corner, not cowards fleeing before a revolution, but redeemers and benefactors, pious aspirants to be noble clay **like lobsters in a mossy tank** under the Almighty effort let us advance on Chaos and **we don't have a shot in** the Dark.

What pretty oracles **sweet babbling brook** nature yields us on this text in the face and behavior of children, babes, and even brutes. That divided and rebel mind, that distrust of a sentiment **you think you have it all figured out** because our arithmetic has computed the strength and means opposed to our purpose, these have not. Their mind being whole, their eye is as yet unconquered **unastonished**, and when we look in their faces, we are disconcerted. Infancy conforms to nobody; all conform to it; **yes;** so that one babe commonly makes four or five out of the adults who prattle and play to it **no tears 'cause you're here**. So God has armed youth and puberty and manhood no less with its own piquancy and charm, and made it enviable and gracious and its claims not to be put by, it will **never, oh god, he will never** stand **breathe** by **on** itself **his own**. Do not think the youth has no force, because he cannot speak to you and me. **I'm listening!** Hark! in the next room who spoke so clear and emphatic? It seems he knows how to speak to his contemporaries. **I'm going out!** Bashful or bold then, he will know how to make us seniors very unnecessary.

The nonchalance of boys who are sure of a dinner **as he always would have been**, and would disdain as much as a lord to do or say aught to conciliate one, is the healthy attitude of human nature. How is a boy the master of society; independent, irresponsible, looking out from his corner on such people and facts as pass by, he tries and sentences them on their merits, in the swift, summary way of boys **is Joe home?**, as good, bad, interesting, silly, eloquent, troublesome. He cumbers himself never about consequences, about interests; he gives an independent, genuine verdict. **There were turkey vultures and a man who sold cracked stones.** You must court him; he does not court you. **He would not sign.** But the man is as it were clapped into jail by his consciousness. **Can you pick me up?** As soon as he has once acted or spoken with eclat he is a committed person, watched by the sympathy or the hatred of hundreds, whose affections must now enter into his account. There is no Lethe for this. **Remember that the fires of hell do not create light like our earthly fires.** Ah, that he could pass again into his neutral, god-like independence! **Regret.** Who can thus lose all pledge and, having observed, observe again from the same unaffected, unbiased, unbribable, unaffrighted innocence **are you the boy's mother?**, must always be formidable, must always engage the poet's **non-trivialities** and the man's regards. Of such an immortal youth the force would be felt, **the taut bounce of a basketball on pavement in the distance**. He would utter opinions on all passing affairs, which being seen to be not private but necessary, would sink like darts into the ear of men and put them in fear. **When he gets where he's going, will the people there be strangers to him?**

These are the voices **voices** which we hear in solitude, but they grow faint and inaudible as we enter into the world. Society everywhere is in conspiracy against the manhood of every one of its members **like sunflowers unturned in the years since they replaced the sun with an artificial star**. Society is a joint-stock company, in which the members agree, for the better securing of his bread to each shareholder, to surrender the liberty and culture of the eater. The virtue in most request is conformity. Self-reliance is its aversion. It loves not realities and creators, but names and customs.

THE BACK HOUSE

when it comes time to
use the knife
I won't flinch and
I won't blame
you

Charles Bukowski

You Drive

when faraway desert suffers locust crisis
who can speak of this year's yield? I sowed
nothing, licensed nothing, studied figures
rhythmic as charcoal sketches of a nude

in this time of inglorious production
I ceded control over my orgasm to no one
but I admit I loved the two-door Civic
its intelligible parts, its idiosyncrasies

The Boiler Room

32

waking later still in the near-total dark
hearing flames click in the metal belly
the moan of the pipes as they expand
the stoic, green LED and the red one

once I was taken to the railroad tracks
their unguarded openness was like this
always maintain a reasonable distance
the locomotive comes around a curve

Hotel Reversible Destiny

two people begin to hate day-to-day intimacy
after some time no eye contact is possible
what otherwise is told by steel: look here—
snowed stables, the rearing aqueduct

intermittent cars washing by like ocean
listen, if you could even call it music
who dares to dream of boundless arches?
the girl at the market opens her robe

Disappearing

34

scrapping copper
from what became

the basement

taught me a void
is made with effort

just wear the gloves
you said

From a Photograph

inside my copy of Oppen's
Selected

there is a photograph

I am always finding
I have hidden

from myself
like this

The Courtyard

years ago the street stank of shit so bad they built a house
behind the house with the basement where you live
    sometimes

though the back house also has a basement where you live
sometimes

where a salmon run of strangers lives
sometimes

stunned by the sun, emerging into the addressless
square

I know both houses are splendid with people
but I don't believe it

I never see anybody there

Strikethrough

The doctor counseled patience
Funerary accumulated sediment
The guts of a vending machine
Humiliating hylic attachment
Held by effigy in scaffolding
Red motorcycle against the snow

I had been sleeping
through the end of the movie
to me, Doughboy did not die
when I awoke speaking aloud
to you, it was of a closer death
tattered, binding

Shift

I begin passing frozen
lakes at such frequency
at such speed, each unlit
northeastern town is ice
tapered in the crevices

I do not find a way
to grieve within the law

Deeper

let me show you the vine that was planted on my birthday
to be exactly as old as a network of fruit creeping slowly
until it consumes the wall, the fenceposts, time peeling
back from the host—what's inside makes nostalgia
look like human defect, fig or grape I think
owning nothing, covering everything
like the ice they told me on my birthday slicked
the courtyard—to be born means nothing
even in January, one year embraced like a lover
the next rung in coldly, kissing each other's cheeks
saying things like I want to see sunlight
today but I won't I'm too tired I'm
growing nonlinearly I miss you already
I'm loling because I was so worried
at night you become a shadow in the cell

Double Jeopardy

a surplus of doors
and a menagerie of locks

a probable fit, pick, tension
wrench, credit card, flathead, ten thousand

combinations, long hours waiting,
a panicked text, fire escape, lowered

ladder, hopped fence, and on your
dashboard, a ski mask—

I knew then
I would be broken into

but I couldn't think of what I had
that you would want

even less, something I would miss
for already I had left everything I loved

in a pile in a kitchen in St. Louis
even the little yellow step stool

The Courtyard

you, living
has something to do with it
how it mauves before a snowstorm
a perfectly isolated cube
lined with plush

Pioneer Days

I said I would, so I do
give you money, clean,
trill at the unfooled baby

you promised it would be
dignified, and it is, and I
struggle not with it

I have another life—

The Courtyard

today I passed through it
twice alone

II.

The Only Plague We Could Not Bear Was Darkness

Whoso would be a man, must be a nonconformist, **violent and prepared**. He who would gather immortal palms must not be hindered by the name of goodness, but must explore if it be goodness. **Righteousness.** Nothing is at last sacred but the integrity of our own mind. **If a house has waste, water, and heating systems, frailties and veins, tenants and electricity, where is the mind?** Absolve you to yourself, **and what key opens it?** and you shall have the suffrage of the world. I remember an answer which when quite young **hooked on phonics** I was prompted to make to a valued adviser who was wont to importune me with the dear old doctrines of the church. **Should I fetch a priest?** On my saying, What have I to do with the sacredness of traditions, if I live **unbaptized** wholly from within? my friend suggested,—"But these impulses **welcoming the stranger** may be from below, not from above." I replied, "They do not seem to me to be such; **no inspiration but divine inscription;** but if I am the devil's **lawful** child, I will live then from the devil." No law can be sacred to me but that of my nature. Good and bad are but names **Liridon*** very readily transferable **Jackie** to that or this **free son**; the only right is **to**

---

* Albanian *liri*: "liberty," less commonly "looseness," "ease."

navigate **by instinct** what is after my constitution **wind on water**; the only wrong what is against it, **jagged cut through the viscera**. A man is to carry himself **chin up** in the presence of all opposition **the world** as if every thing were titular **existing in title only** and ephemeral **briefly evidenced** but he. I am ashamed to think how easily we capitulate to badges and names, to large societies and dead institutions. Every decent and well-spoken individual affects and sways me more than is right, **ignore the peanut gallery.** I ought to go upright and vital, and speak the rude truth in all ways. If malice and vanity wear the coat of philanthropy, shall that **always** pass **for more**? If an angry bigot assumes this bountiful cause of Abolition, **socioeconomic reasons**, and comes to me with his last news from Barbadoes, why should I not say to him, "Go love thy **ailing** infant; love thy **industrial** wood-chopper; be good-natured and modest; **bring death to the forest never stolen from your fathers and now your own**; have that grace **and proud stride**; and never varnish your hard, uncharitable ambition with this incredible tenderness for black folk a thousand miles off. Thy love afar is spite at home." Rough and graceless **Narcan** would be such greeting, but truth is handsomer than the affectation of love. Your goodness must have some edge to it,—else it is none. **You are caught in the penumbra; I stand in darkness or full light.** The doctrine of hatred must be preached, as the counteraction **lex talionis** of the doctrine of love, when that pules and whines. I shun father and mother and **common-law** wife and brother when my genius calls me. I would write on the lintels of the doorpost, Whim. I hope it is somewhat better than whim at last, but we cannot spend the day in explanation.

Expect me not to show cause why I seek or why I exclude company. **I do whatever I want.** Then, again, do not tell me, as a good man did today, of my obligation to put all poor men in good situations. Are they my poor? **Charity until emergency.** I tell thee, thou foolish philanthropist, **of martial law and continuity of government,** that I grudge the dollar, the dime, the cent I give to such men as do not belong to me and to whom I do not belong. There is a class of persons to whom by all spiritual affinity I am bought and sold; **men harnessing the sun in their acreages, dreaming of sovereignty;** for them I will go to prison if need be; but your miscellaneous popular charities; the education at college of fools; the building of meeting-houses to the vain end to which many now stand; alms to sots, and the thousandfold Relief Societies;—though I confess with shame I sometimes succumb and give the dollar, it is a wicked dollar, which by-and-by I shall have the manhood to withhold. **Fear me.**

Virtues are **held by the poet who turns over and over the glass paperweight, not much to speak of** in the popular estimate, rather the **sort of** exception than the **sort of** rule. There is the man and his **strengths** virtues. Men do what is called a good action **check on Rose,** as some piece of courage or charity **bring Rose grapes,** much as they would pay a fine **enter your license plate number** in expiation of daily non-appearance on **an Independence Day** parade **in West Texas, where children mounted on ATVs and horses know what they celebrate better than their parents.** Their **parents'** works are done as an apology or extenuation **minimization** of their living **impact** in the world,—as invalids and the insane pay a high board **so it is safest never to let them see you cry.** Their virtues are penances **because I didn't do anything**. I do not wish to expiate, but to live. My life is not an apology, but a life. It is for itself and not for a spectacle **unless I can interest you in some dessert**. I much prefer that it should be of a lower strain **handwash only**, so it be genuine and equal **I hunt, you kill**, than that it should be glittering **like the fig tree in the dewy greenhouse** and unsteady **in the winter months**. I wish it to be sound and sweet, and not to need diet and bleeding **should resume within twelve weeks or consult a doctor**. My life should be unique, **heightened**; it should be an alms **not a tax**, a battle **pyrrhic**, a conquest **in a bedroom in December**, a medicine **that erases your memory of pain but does nothing to numb it, fooling the body into trying again**. I ask primary evidence that you are a man **let me see your hands**, and refuse this appeal from the man to his actions. I know that for myself it makes no difference whether I do or forbear those actions which are reckoned excellent. I cannot consent to pay for a privilege where I have intrinsic right. Few and mean as my gifts may be, I actually am **standing here, the one you love, right in front of you**, and do not need for my own assurance or the assurance of my fellows any secondary testimony.

What I must do is all that concerns me, not what the people think **you make a horrible mistake; you trust the wrong person; you choose to save yourself and someone more vulnerable dies**. This rule **firstborn son**, equally arduous **the only plague we could not bear was darkness** in actual **frogs** and in intellectual **lice** life, may serve **blood in the water** for the whole **boils** distinction **locusts** between greatness **hail** and meanness **pestilence, hordes of wild animals**. It is the harder because you will always find those who think they know what is your duty better **firstborn son** than you know it **darkness**. It is easy in the world to live after the world's opinion; it is easy in solitude to live after our own; but the great man is he who in the midst of the crowd keeps with perfect sweetness the independence of solitude.*

The objection to conforming **held by all adolescents** to usages that have become dead to you is that it scatters your force, **if you are unable to speak back to time**. It loses your **newness, if you figure yourself without relation to** time and blurs the impression of your character **three days old and already so serious**. If you maintain a dead church **Quaker graveyard**, contribute to a dead Bible **for a more hopeful** Society, vote with a great party **Friday night** either for the Government or against it, spread your table **with eerie cards in diagonal relation to each other** like base housekeepers **women**,—under all these screens I have difficulty **when I am at my desk** to detect **suss out** the precise man you are **going crazy since the moment I met you**. And of course so much force is withdrawn from your proper life, **to be out on**

---

* If you found the note on my iPad, you never spoke of it.
I wrote myself fleeing the scene, arms full of artifacts.
I denied regression toward the mean. Yellow reams say
that was not the worst of it. Twirling darkly on the rink
I thought I saw a pair refusing chocolate, touch, moving
separately across the ice. It was just us. Your name appears
in solid ink on the line *after death, will to*. I should be fluent
in projecting myself onto a screen by now, or imminently...
The country priest diaries about a horrible stomachache
and something horned steps into the world, hunched,
determined to finish it. Don't ask me where I was
in the days before the scaffold, apparently untouched,
came down. Ignore the racy shifting in the mirror.
Headlit, the pale animal runs off, into the interior.

the town in the polluted city, not swimming with the eels and plucking the fruits of your birthright. But do your thing **thang**, and I shall **always** know you. Do your work, and you shall reinforce yourself **like any king, mighty and decorated but subject to his subjects.** A man must consider **the cost** what a blindman's buff **why lie** is this game of conformity **the ante.** If I know your **intersect**ion I **do my best not to** anticipate your argument. I hear a preacher announce for his text **fie!** and topic the expediency of one of the institutions of his church **in a world where everything is in question.** Do I not know beforehand **plain slice not too hot please** that not possibly can he say a new and spontaneous word? **I won't go to services if there's singing.** Do I not know that with all this ostentation of examining the grounds of the institution he will do no such thing? **Don't look back.** Do I not know that he is pledged to himself not to look but at one side, the permitted side, not as a man, but as a parish minister? **Turns to salt.** He is a retained attorney **in a windowless office in midtown,** and these airs of the bench are the emptiest affectation. Well, most men have bound their eyes with one or another handkerchief **burden,** and attached themselves to some one of these communities of opinion. This conformity makes them not false in a few particulars, authors of a few lies, but false in all particulars. **Man lives to project himself outward, for better or worse.** Their every truth is not quite true. **He had one foot out the door already.** Their two is not the real two, their four not the real four: so that every word they say chagrins **wearies** us and we know not where to begin to set them right. **When it comes to the value of literature, we simply cannot see eye to eye.** Meantime nature is not slow to equip us in the prison-uniform of the **pharmaceutical** party to which we adhere. We come to wear one cut of face and figure, and acquire by **withholding** degrees the gentlest asinine expression. There is a mortifying experience in particular, which does not fail to wreak itself also in the general history; I mean "the **supplicant's** foolish face of praise," the forced smile which we put on in company where we do not feel at ease, in answer to conversation which does not interest us. The muscles, not spontaneously moved but moved by a low usurping wilfulness, grow tight about the outline of the face, and make the most disagreeable sensation; a sensation of rebuke and warning which no brave young man will suffer twice. **Instead of a fence, the poet said, we planted bamboo, and look how quickly it's come up.**

THE SQUINT

For now we see through a glass, darkly; but then face
to face: now I know in part; but then shall I know even
as also I am known.

1 Corinthians 13:12

The world
Through a window
& with me
The lepers & vices
The sighs & belches
The tragically ill
The condemned & frozen
Raynaud & Down

All of us
Correspondents
The cordoned-off
We train our eyes on the vicars
Spectacled & drowned

& so poisoned
So radoned
So fulfilled
So
Intramuscular
& burdened
& so neurotypically
Felled

& the altos catch the drift
& so degrades all living analysis
The broken rubber seals
All the leaks & pipe fittings
& all immodesties
From where I peer
Through the lychnoscope
I see

I go down beneath
Where the smoke issues
I wake up conductive
Arguing with a roach over
Which of us owns
My fucking sandwich
I wake up in nests
Infinitely breached
Bleeding (hissing
Loudly expanding, ah
No it's just the radiator)

I go down beneath
I crawl through the metal bull
Which is the entire project's
Boiler
The source of all heat
& all lies

& inside the belly
Of this gigantic manmade whale
There is a squint, too

But through it one sees
Only fire
Though currently
Not
Sent here
As I was
To reignite the pilot

Darkened
I see the stamps passing
Hand to hand
The test strips
& pneumatic tubes
Puppy pads
& numerous other synthetics
By which one sees into the Eyes of Loneliness

Which are by the way
Not your eyes

Don't worry

Through the lychnoscope
One sees still
What one might expect
The Chalice & its Appurtenances
But the man who raises it
To his lips—drinks

Each of us has done
Something unspeakable
To be here

Though it appears
That those who would observe the altar
Freely, unencumbered
By our jailhouse window
Have already moved on
& so, at the Chalice
We are the only ones left looking

From the Squint
I see a horrible flatland

The
Man
Sacrifice
Bird
Arrowhead
Sandwich

The one whose death commands
Hundreds more

& the one who makes none
Into eternity supporting him

& then the story is sugarscrubbed
Which undoes nothing

& they are gone a generation
Before the settlers arrive

Who is with me?
I am alone, but
Uniquely accompanied
The air I breathe is controlled
By a switch—switch
Would turn to fire
All the air & then
Every molecule inside me
There's a man standing by that switch
We have worked together for years
We have gotten drunk many times
We nearly speak each other's languages
My safety is of
No small concern to him
Yet I am the one in the belly
It is my turn

Ornamentation on the hull of a ship
A violent story borne out in carvings
We've waited seasons to be confirmed

In the beliefs we had about the ones who
Chiseled us from hematite so jokingly
We laugh less looking at the moraine

The glacial tracks on God's arm
They may dance, but we're stuck on this
Cruiseline—this time, to watch them

Raise the form, spilling barnacles & sewage
Overhead bursts the snowy owl
The final dream of a captured spirit

Ends, the canal just ahead, darkly lit
Before it is dragged ashore by the harbormen
& hauled to the 24-hour scrapyard

& then the service becomes terribly loud

But before
When it ferried souls on less than holy rivers
I crawled through the hatch & through the porthole
Saw the enormous mechanical octopus
& felt it score the soft metal underbelly:
Death, in the impossible depths beneath, & joy
& language marked in passing—but then
Another ship went by & I saw you
Looking through your lychnoscope

Later on, we arrived in America
& a long time went by of frozen cotton
& then we awoke one August in a box store parking lot
& around us dozens of men still slept in their trucks
& a woman rolled shopping carts in preparation to open
& there were no voids or bayous, nowhere to go
Except inside, where air was frigid & penetrative
& among the aisles, there could be no lychnoscope

The building feels me squirm in its belly
& shivers with pleasure

The old thermocouple lies dead in my hand
& the bright replacement in my pocket

Sings out—

Suspended in the darkness for three days
(Forget the journeys of ritual initiates:

Three days to perish of thirst, or
To blossom & pass from the uterus)

The thermocouple joins me
To various necrotic appointments

Visits all the public places
The kernel of life, yet undetonated

Watches a robbery on the deli television
& conspires precociously

& sleeps, mostly, preparing for a day
Of sudden & incredible voltage

Solar Inverter

A correction note to a mysterious entity:
it is not just the days, but the presences
which are growing longer. Bound by wire
to the roof, the brick chimney dissembling,
I speak a language understood by cats,
birds, and the irrational. I begin to fear,
like all animated things, the imminent,
the inevitable, terribly: the unbridled
loosed upon the world, the escape
of spirits I've gathered into me.

There is a fault in my manufacturing.
There is a bulb that does not flicker
because it was born dead, neither green
nor intervallic. No human can know
if I am powered on without listening.
To circuitry I become the intolerable
answer, the blind path, where eventually
man, mineral, and electricity are one,
the loop closed by my master's fleshy
hand, the hideous moment of joining—

III.

To Stand Still in a Vortex

Despite the best of intentions all around, for non-conformity the world whips you with its displeasure. And therefore **fairly or unfairly** a man must know how to estimate a sour face **and argumentative gesture**. The bystanders **neighbor walking the dog** look askance on him in the public street **36 hours of hollering** or in the friend's parlor. If this aversation had its origin in contempt **don't touch me** and resistance like his own he might well go home with a sad countenance; but the sour faces of the multitude **ants on a log**, like their sweet faces, have no deep cause **wet black bough**—disguise no **benevolent** god, but are put on and off as the wind blows and a newspaper directs **us to stand still in a vortex**. Yet is the discontent of the multitude **evacuation order** more formidable than that of the senate and the college **lambs to the cosmic slaughter**. It is easy enough for a firm man **midwit** who knows the world to brook **bleed the dam** the rage of the cultivated classes. Their rage is decorous and prudent, for they are timid, as being very vulnerable themselves. But when to their feminine rage **try me** the indignation of the people is added, when the ignorant and the poor are aroused **violent and prepared**, when the unintelligent brute force **masculinity** that lies at the bottom of society **sadism** is made to growl and meow, it needs the habit of magnanimity and religion to treat it godlike as a trifle of no concernment.

The other terror **data** that scares us from self-trust is our **heartbroken** consistency; a reverence for our past act or word **etched in stone** because the eyes of others have no other data **input** for computing our **widening** orbit **spiral** than our past acts **works**, and we are loath to disappoint them. **If it were me, I might never write again.**

But why should you keep your head over your shoulder? **What choice do I have?** Why drag about this monstrous corpse of your memory, lest you contradict **revise** somewhat you have stated in this or that public place? Suppose you should contradict yourself; what then? It seems to be a rule of wisdom never to rely on your memory **photographs** alone, scarcely even in acts of pure memory, **hypermnesia is a disorder**, but to bring the past for judgment into the thousand eyed present **vanishing twin**, and live ever in a new day. **Remember to forget.** Trust your emotion. In your **parthenogenic** metaphysics **(that is to say, fatherless)** you have denied personality to the **mythomaniacal** Deity, yet when the devout **ascetic** motions of the soul come **zero-cal**, yield to them **the** heart and life **ouroboros**, though they should clothe **fleece** God with shape and **prismatic** color. Leave your **little** theory **swaddled in a white sheet**, as Joseph his coat in the hand of the harlot, and flee **like it was nothing.**

A foolish consistency is the hobgoblin of little minds, adored by little statesmen **I build it, you sweep it** and **half-understood** philosophers and **re**-divines. With consistency a great soul has simply nothing to do **and must spend some time horizontal, recovering in front of the tube.** He may as well concern himself with his shadow

ducks and nuns on the wall. Out upon your guarded lips! Sew them up with packthread, do. Else if you would be a man speak what you think today in words as hard as cannon balls, and tomorrow speak **where you at** what tomorrow thinks **I'll be there in twenty** in hard words again **tell me what happened**, though it contradict every thing you said today. Ah, then, exclaim the aged ladies, you shall be sure to be misunderstood! Misunderstood! It is a right fool's word. Is it so bad then to be misunderstood? Pythagoras' **wife** was misunderstood, and Socrates' **wife**, and Jesus' **wife**, and Luther's **wife**, and Copernicus **you get it**, and Galileo **thought comets were an optical illusion**, and Newton **died drinking mercury**, and every pure and wise spirit **I knew** that ever took flesh **was made to eat it later on**. To be greatly **influenced by men** is to be misunderstood **as in their service**.

I suppose no man can **help but** violate his nature. All the sallies of his will are rounded in by the law **as fat, white, and violent as the judge of the desert, as the co**incidence of his being, as the inequalities of Andes and Himmaleh are insignificant **spikes** in the curve of the sphere. Nor does it matter **anything you will ever do again**, how you gauge **love** and try **to recall** him. A character **shaped like a mouth unsounding** is like an acrostic **sobriquet** or **neatly stitched** Alexandrian stanza;—read it! forward, backward, or across, it still spells the same thing. In this pleasing contrite **implacable** wood-life which God **cheekily** allows me, let me record day by day my honest thought without prospect **street, where we grew up**, or retrospect, **without avarice**, and I cannot doubt, it will be found symmetrical, though I mean it not and see it not. **In a world where everyone is a twin,**

are you the evil one? My book should smell of pines and resound with the hum of insects. The swallow over my window should interweave that thread or straw he carries in his bill into my web also. We **can only hope to** pass for what we are. Character teaches above our wills. Men imagine **themselves on the moon** that they communicate their **pitiful** virtue or vice only by overt actions, and do not see that virtue or vice emit a breath every moment. **Is he sedated? No.**

Fear never **always** but **for some reason** you shall be consistent in whatever variety of actions **walking and chewing gum,** so they be each honest and natural in their hour. For of one will, the actions will be **sleazy and** harmonious, however unlike they seem. These **teeming** varieties are lost sight of when seen at a little distance, at a little height of thought. One tendency unites them all, **to kneel in awe of God's terrible face.** The voyage of the best ship is a zigzag line of a hundred tacks. This is only microscopic criticism. See the line **snipped** from a sufficient distance, and it straightens itself to the average tendency. Your genuine action will explain itself and will explain your other genuine actions. Your conformity explains nothing. Act singly, and what you have already done singly will justify you now. Greatness always appeals to the future. If I can be great enough now to do right and scorn eyes, I must have done so much right before as to defend me now. **Move within the physical constraints of the universe, but outside its law.** Be it how it will, do right now. **Have a way with animals.** Always scorn appearances and you always may. The force of character is cumulative. All the foregone days of virtue work their **thin-fingered** health into this. What makes the majesty of the heroes of the senate **what?** and the **poetics of the open** field, which so fills the imagination? The **taurine** consciousness of a train of great days and victories behind **bores me absolutely to death.** There they all stand and shed an united light on the advancing actor. He is attended as by a visible escort of angels **in a room unknown** to every man's eye. That is it which throws thunder **underonerungungodgivenplunderun-motherunwonderundrivenbridgeownerunmore** into Chatham's voice, and dignity into Washington's **cup of** port, and America into Adams's **glass** eye **and dentures.** Honor is venerable **vegetable** to us because it is no **ex-cuse me** ephemeris. It is always ancient virtue **he cites when explaining why he won't do a very simple thing.** We worship it today **laundry** because it is not of today **dishes.** We love it **mopping** and pay it **folding** homage because it is not a trap for our love **don't even start with the shopping and cooking** and **worst of all, the** homage, but is self-dependent **I choose,** self-derived **I make my-self,** and therefore **it keeps us going in the way** of an old immaculate pedigree, even if shown in a **I was once a** young person.

I hope in these **woebegone** days we have heard the last of conformity and consistency **and that soon we will come to believe everything happens for a reason.** Let the words be gazetted and ridiculous henceforward. In-stead of the gong for dinner, let us hear a whistle from the Spartan fife. Let us bow and apologize never more. A great man is coming to eat at my house. I do not wish to please him: I wish that he should wish to please me. I will stand here **on the precipice** for humanity, and though I would make it kind **of not exactly the way it is,** I would make it truer. Let us affront **He who spurned me** and reprimand the smooth mediocrity **the bureaucracy of death** and squalid contentment of the times **when I defy the limit**, and hurl in the face of custom and trade and office, the fact which is the upshot of all history, that there is a great responsible **culpable** Thinker and Actor moving **against the light** wherever moves a man; that a true man belongs to no other time or place, but is the centre of things, **and in his presence I am nothing but a cold and distant moon.** Where he is, there is **no** nature, **for nature moves. Though he speaks no judgment,** he measures you and all men and all events. You are constrained to accept his standard **unchanged as he is unchanged.** Ordinarily, every **harboring** body in society reminds us of somewhat else, or of some other person, **the irrecoverable smell of travel.** Character **in his new shoulders**, reality, reminds you of nothing else; it takes place of the whole creation. The man must be so much that he must make all circumstances indifferent—put all means into the shade, **and disappear into the void.** This all great men are and do. Every true man is a cause, a country, and an age; requires infinite spaces and numbers and time fully to accomplish his thought;—and posterity seem to follow his steps as a procession. A man Cæsar is born **eight pounds six ounces**, and for ages after we have a Roman Empire. Christ is born, and millions of minds so grow and cleave to his genius that he is confounded with virtue and the possible of man **and then betrayed and scourged and murdered and God, who was able to bear every other parent's weeping, realizes it is time to change the rules entirely.**

Adjustment You Walk Away Again

"You're nice." You're late. Your voice. We have to get
rid of them. Our most private moments. Never spoken
of. Never written down. This is the sleep of kings.

Ray DiPalma, Charles Bernstein

What do the ruins think?
Flashblindness—

Permanent eclipse
Setting silently evacuated

The law of shock says
No

Then there is a filling of the space
Between the viscera

Blown apart stone
Dies where the fig tree was

My doppelgänger trawls the neighborhood for weakness

Litigious dawn the animals the greenhouse

No but now the clarity of the worried lip
The deluded gesture cracking chestnuts
Who lies dormant at the bottom of the stairs
In the dark? To have gracefully ministered
The shutdown sequence of guest rooms
Only to trip on the quiet the hollow
Which ingratiates night into itself

What it expels freezes almost instantly
Caught in the air between us like a yell
Gored by hooves the morning expressively
Slips from my hands and mind replaced
By the time I think it most often was
Noonish when we worked the races
November breaking behind our line

Like any other month before accounted
By irregular computers shirking cursive
I elaborate at least partially for the purpose
Of data entry rasping analysis of the guts
Of the building which I was told could not
Think only act and feel and feel materially
But there are many ways to ingest manioc

Rhododendron spikes elevators mortuary
I looked into the theater and saw a novel
Color spilled on the floor told to be patient
Riddled deeply smoking staring at nothing
From the porch it appeared to be November
Though it had been recuperating for some time
No but now the wall has been completely

The inflamed median hosts stiff grass
As the weight of too many rests on me
A sort of lens that glaze that predictable harkening
Even ears feel leaden when the sinkhole opens
So still I sit it does not know I fear it

I move past the present into the certainty of cooling
    infinitives
Suspend my gaze on laths and derivatives
On the cattail marsh circumambulated
By childhood's footsteps inscribed by what
A time to be alive the billowing year of zero magnitude

When it could be said the future was obvious and trained
Like the loyalty of the falcon to sleeved meat
There was something about the economy
Stumbling as it created sensuous and wilder
Fools for love that made us all prone to gambling

Of rabbits in stillness I dreamed repeatedly
Their movement in another time signature
Gray on green on the day no wind dared

Like a river rich in time trout moved invisibly beneath us
Without concealing the afternoon on shitbed creek
When characterization split like a diamond uncorrupted
Wintry symmetry tied us to the banister: two shores
One soul of a blind alley and one of little jewels
Too diurnal to transgress the bedroom
Too much art and no cinder light to read by
Intuition a blameless advance in a bear hunt
That next year there would be different arms

Speak of the end and then of the beginning

Anchored to light poles the handwritten signs become
frantic and shameless *PORPHYRY LASTS FOR EVER
LIKE ALL ANTHEMS AND ALL MY CORPORATE
STRUCTURES LOST*

DOG

In the gale bloodless tile holds its
Mercury though I
Step out onto it only rarely

For this place is not my home
I do not trust it to be free of glass

I have seen it shatter into particles
Suspended in the air achieved in the lungs

It is too late to falter in our walk into the eyes

We ascend the stairs then cling to the rungs

Satiate the bee in her warm home with a little soda

Shoulder surface in the springlight annealing

Razed, the rooms kissed last show no sign

Holy we cross the rooftops no building ours

Nor could be owned except by cleaving

Except by hands alight on lumbar holy

Soda fizzing black in her tiny fixtured eyes

For weeks I did not come down from the drug of sudden absence, the hours it opens, the lonely door of the office after midnight which I loved, sudden hunger. As before, I knew I would not see what I had adored again. When the trains came I was always on them and when malfunctioning zones of the city sprouted archways impossibly quickly I walked through looking up. The sky bit as it does in winter. Someone knit a formless shrug. The freezing wave bore a tremendous dead seagull so I switched to vodka with ice.

Far away a body receded tamely and was molded into a sort of park, with runners, dogs, and teenagers, slowpokes and war memorials, its shrunken wild mortgaged to a nationwide mall conglomerate. I had been keeping up with this online and in the paper and was not surprised when one day my mind simply wouldn't start. Whom to call? The tremendous white corpse floated north to the sound where I'd been told constellations could still be seen, but they took the form of children's drawings, bland in their figurativeness unless they're a portrait of you.

Migrating grackles forget and circle
At the end of the week it snows
I turn heart years old poinsettia
Years cabled across vast distances
Into the self, away from the birds

Beckett's naked woman in a shrinking box
Takes a position called the seed
Vertex pressed to knees for reaching
Into the heart, away from the words

Speak Open the Perimeter

Fewer hypothermic casualties
In the new weather

Fishkill at Wolf's Point
In the red ocean

Figures lean from windows
In January whispermist

Dampness and illness
Nightfall on the perimeter

Everyone starts having terrifying nightmares at the
    same time

This fucks with everyone exactly as much as you'd
    think

I'd been mad before but now I was scared

Besides the vague arachnid shadow, most everyone is
    able to shrug it off by noon

Prairie flat afternoon dimidiated by coffee and alcohol

Rust rattling in the underbody, diesel fume in the
    hayfield, blurred house

Everyone swears off coffee and then alcohol

Nothing ever happens but it never stops

The writing is adjourned for ten days
Always with us, too fearful to approach
More cat than witch more throat than airy
Soundscape of the cold which cannot exist
As if air had been made so one could hear
As if I had been made so I could hear
Its song
                    Desolate horse at the fence
                                              Angler's
Line in the water dragging death and mud
Water and it hurts, pulls against expansion
Like a hair elastic northwind of the burbs
Child at the screen door   no child
At the screen door
Ragged breath   no child

Address: easy to discover: input
A pair of quotation marks, maintain
A sense of finality in detail, the indefinite
Brokered away with
Certainty, I am I, the
Debt is the
Debt
Everyone can use this restroom
Finding you
Generates terraria of misery
Glistening ecologies
Handheld son before the house (street view)
I spawn and spawn again
Just out of century they rebuild the park
Jailed boats line its newborn shore
Jade meadows stay jade, fathers
Jog weekly in it
Kayak runoff
Limey with industrial laminate
Mist, a chord shivers in the mist
No one calls, no one
Opens mail while accusing
Postal workers of theft or idiocy
Quarrels do not flare except in the county's
Quiet courts, or during
Quaint midnight spousal burnings
Query: how far away is the farthest place on earth?
Racially remixed every decade, the township
Ratifies a set of laws later found to be
Superunconstitutional
Such as: without a tag to prove your residence
The streets are off limits: you could be

Ticketed or worse
Traffic really had come to such a level
Understand that such a mind, capable of anything but
        interested only in the
Ugliest of slurs, can never succeed in moving away
Ur-states of pain and exhaustion limit possibility,
        contrary to what you might think
Vague bridges in the fog tell you where you are if you
        pretend to be lost
Violence done here has a way of not following you home,
        that I'll
Verify: I understand the
Wild usefulness of such a habitat, I
Would wager its crepuscular shroud and
Weed smoke smell keep it from recurring at
X-rated moments which would have frightened, if you had
XXXXXXX'd while XXX while we were XXXXXXX
Yes we could have chosen somehow else, but there is
Zero so-called logic to that now, just as there is
Zero chance of returning the shattered
Zygote to life, just as there is
Zero chance the horse at the fence is a
Zebra

Cruelty Bores Me

But its masks offer endless pleasure
Changed, the future looks back in terror
Endowed with hips, curve, the future
At once blush pink and the color of grass
When free dances, when captured vanishes
Sultry, invisible, deathmasklike, diaphanous

The Sadistic License of Privacy

Though I knew it could not exist, I craved a canonical version, some XML to dig my teeth into, automated instances unfailingly rendered with every error grandfathered in. Though I knew it could not exist, I defined attributions plastic enough to accept varieties of inputs without putting garbage back into the world. Though I knew it could not exist, I mediated the limitless with structures capacious enough to hold it, backrooms, iced blacktops, and so on, parent classes, child classes, spent and loaded placeguns. Though I knew it could not exist, I made a book of all things and then, of course, overwrote it. Though I knew it could not exist, the inevitability of some contrasting with the coincidence of others became a value judgment, but not to me. For I knew I could not hope to understand this never mind explain it, all I can do is reproduce it perfectly.

Sparrows Importance

The high wind at night is hardly erotic
Tipped plate store glass, shimmering
Earthquake country, breaking things,
Foreign thorns surmount their fences
Protrude into the road where we will
Never go, never walk together, like
Nights we never went, never walked
Together, for connected by a chain
So delicate in light it seems coolly
Liquid, you and I and homeland
Pull back, enslave each other

Ball

They race toward the line I stand on.
Then they are arguing around me

and laughing too. They hoop,
they enact a living, they say

the season ends too soon.
Like the winter beyond the Aprils

paint at the court lines
gaps in the overlight.

Beeline

Everyone told us the thing about bees.
Everyone told us we'd move through it
like sand, but no one said what sand moves like.

The house, ours for the night, had a hole
at its center, large as a room.
Only when I pulled back the curtain

was the extent of the damage revealed to us,
the colorful lengths gone to sustain the fiction
more alarming than the cold. In my shoes

there was an indefinite amount of sand
but an absolute number of grains. Everyone
told us there was more than we could count

but you can count, in fact you must. Our grammar
requires counting. We went out and stood
on the precipice we call the coast.

Walkthrough

As I am unable to imagine
that the dragon has shadow
powers, or double damage
powers, I am prohibited
from the subtle striking of the
left and right buttons
which at particular moments
seems as much a skill as
the ratchet or the good knife
require, and because I cannot
see myself as prince of any land
I become the voice of the guide.
The only path through fire,
hedges, the undersea level
becomes apparent through me.
What was play becomes
more similar to a march
over acrid tundra, ending
(make no mistake, ending)
the way we knew it would
having seen the end screen
long ago, in childhood.
If I seem reluctant to heft
the sword, even the book
of spells, it is because I know
the answers, honestly or not.
I can't let you go into the cave
without a way out.

Hellgrammite

It occurred in two phases:
quiet years of the life aquatic
then flight, for just a few hours,
before I died on the foamy shelf
overlooking my bag of offspring.
To the dark water I reluctantly
return, over the worn stones
home where I am called, like
all my kind, back into sand,
the substance of our history.
Some of the dead are winged.
Some are not. I do not care,
I do not remember. The past's
weight crushes my carapace.
I did not know love, only
blindness. I ate animals
much larger than myself,
moved in the shadows,
attacked a human child.
There was no redemption
but job security: visitors
wandering in from the light,
whose voices rang and stung,
never forgot the sight of us.
We grew huge in the riverbed.

IV.

Listless Monuments in the Shape of Temples Fall

An institution is **no longer** the lengthened shadow of one man; as, the Reformation, of Luther; Quakerism, of Fox; Methodism, of Wesley; Abolition, of Clarkson. Scipio, Milton called "the height of Rome;" **all these and more we had, but we don't know what happened to them and that said, it is still true that** all history resolves itself very easily into the biography of a few stout and **less than** earnest persons.

Let a man then know his worth **infinite to me, my love**, and keep things under his feet. Let him not peep or steal, or skulk up and down with the air of a charity-boy, a bastard **would they ever have called you that?**, or an interloper in the world which exists for him—**but you were an antelope between the world and me**. But the man in the street, finding no worth in himself which corresponds to the force which built a tower or sculptured a marble god, feels poor when he looks at these. To him a palace, a statue, or a costly book have an alien and forbidding air, much like a gay equipage, and seem to say like that, 'Who are you, sir?' Yet they all are his **inheritance**, suitors for his notice, petitioners to his faculties that they will come out and take possession. **The trick would be to raise him so he did not feel entitled to the work of others.** The picture waits **unsettled** for my verdict; it is not to command me, but I am to settle its claim to praise. **The infant, the artist, traveling beyond the call of his mother's voice, cocks his head up at her but does not reply, as if to say, I will not be commanded.** That popular fable of the sot who was picked up dead drunk in the street, carried to the duke's house, washed and dressed and laid in the duke's bed, and, on his waking, treated with all obsequious ceremony like the duke, and assured that he had been insane—owes its popularity to the fact that it symbolizes so well the state of man, who **thinks if it walks like a duke it must be a duke,** is in the world a sort of sot, but now and then wakes up, exercises his reason and finds himself a true prince.

To begin again, our reading is mendicant and sycophantic. In history **there would soon be a louder child** our imagination makes fools of us, plays us false. Kingdom and lordship, power and estate, are a gaudier vocabulary than private John and Edward in a small house and common day's work: but the things of life are the same to both: the sum total of both is the same. Why all this deference to Alfred and Scanderbeg and Gustavus **if all that is made manifest is made so by light**? Suppose they were virtuous; did they wear out virtue? As great a stake depends on your private act today as followed their public and renowned steps. When private men shall act with original views, the lustre will be transferred from the actions of kings to those of gentlemen **while a woman should always know when she's not wanted.**

The world has indeed been instructed by its kings, who have so magnetized **in colorful bursts** the eyes of nations. It has been taught by this colossal **agate** symbol the mutual reverence that is due from man to man.

The joyful loyalty with which men have everywhere suffered the king, the noble, or the great proprietor to walk among them by a law of his own, make his own scale of men and things and reverse theirs, pay for benefits not with money but with honor, and represent the Law in his person, was the hieroglyphic by which they obscurely signified their consciousness of their own right and comeliness, the right of every man. **As we continue, I hope you will be less and less moved by the theological-political model.**

The magnetism which all original action exerts is explained **pelvic rest** when we inquire the reason of self-trust **so I will not be lifting any eighty pound bags of concrete.** Who is the Trustee? **Are you in there?** What is the aboriginal **beansprout** Self, on which a universal reliance may be grounded? What is the nature and power of that science-baffling star, **I was most impressed with the canticles of ions** without parallax, without calculable elements **which cause people all over the world to fall in love with my calculator,** which shoots a ray of beauty **order** even into trivial and impure actions, if the least mark of **artificial general** independence appear? The inquiry leads us to that source, at once the essence **ipseity** of genius, the essence of virtue, and the essence of life, which we call Spontaneity or Instinct. We denote this primary wisdom as **mother's** Intuition **which at least in my case could hardly be said to exist,** whilst all later teachings are tuitions, **if we could afford it.** In that deep **pulling** force, the last **uterine** fact behind which analysis cannot go, all things find their common origin **and what do you know, third time in three years.** For the sense of being which in calm hours **porchlight** rises, we know not how, in the soul, is not diverse from **disparate** things, from space from light, from time **shed here**, from man **squeezing my arm with an assessing hand**, but one with them and proceedeth obviously from the same source whence their life and being also proceedeth. We first share the life by **crying out, later we discuss** which things exist and afterwards see them as appearances in nature and forget that we have shared their cause. Here is the **illuminated cerulean** fountain of action and **here is** the fountain **brimming with black goo** of thought. Here are the lungs of that inspiration **perhaps they'd gotten coated** which giveth man wisdom, of that inspiration **spark** of man which cannot be denied without impiety and atheism. We lie in the lap of immense intelligence, which makes us organs of its activity and receivers of its truth. When we discern **what doesn't feel like** justice, when we discern **ineluctable** truth, we do nothing of **consequence** ourselves, but allow a passage to its beams **merging and dehiscing over time.** If we ask whence this comes **while all I care about is one line: heartbeat**, if we seek to pry into the soul that causes—all metaphysics, all philosophy is at fault, **nothing more absurd than** *cogito ergo sum*. Its presence or its absence is all we can affirm. Every man discerns **chooses the best chicken wing** between the voluntary acts of his mind and his involuntary perceptions. And **strips it of extra breading,** to his involuntary perceptions he knows a perfect respect is due **as well as the cat, who always gets her mouthful.** He may err in the expression of them, but he knows that these things are so, like day and night, not to be disputed. All my wilful **beastly** actions and **gross** acquisitions are but roving **as the hot air balloon over the plain over which I failed to provide safe passage;**—the most trivial **no** reverie, the faintest native emotion **no**, are domestic **which is not synonymous with tame** and divine **until you really see what you are looking at**. Thoughtless people **have no self to lose** contradict as readily the statement of perceptions as of opinions, or rather much more readily; for they do not distinguish between perception and notion **but it is not clear what self offers at this point**. They fancy that I choose to see this or that thing. But perception is not whimsical, but fatal **attraction**. If I see a trait, my children **Ismail** will see it after me, and in course of time all mankind,—although it may chance that no one has seen it before me. For my perception of it is as much a fact as the sun.

The relations of the soul to the divine spirit are so pure that it is profane to seek **to interfere** to interpose helps. It must be that when God speaketh he should communicate, not one thing, but all things; should fill the world with his voice; should scatter forth light, nature, time, souls, from the **bulging** centre of the present thought; and new date and new create the whole **linea nigra**. Whenever a mind is simple and receives a divine wisdom, then old things pass away,—means, teachers, texts, **listless monuments in the shape of** temples fall*;

----

*   too many shadows. I can't
   look. I hear a man strike a child
   through evening indigo, through
   the screened living window.
   the immaculate house breeds
   darkened images like these
   the donkey writhing on its back,
   my parents. the incandescent mass
   hovers just beneath, outside
   my vision but within my reach
   but no voice speaks to me.

it lives now, and absorbs past and future into the present hour. All things are made sacred by relation to it,—one thing as much as another. **Living three seconds in the future gives a feeling of perpetual slow motion.** All things are dissolved to their centre by their cause, and in the universal miracle petty and particular miracles disappear. This is **and isn't** and must be **and why not**. If therefore a man claims to know and speak of God and carries you backward to the phraseology of some old mouldered nation in another country **around the time of the split in dialects**, in another world, believe him not. Is the acorn better than the oak which is its fulness and completion? Is the parent better than the child into whom he has cast his ripened being? Whence then this worship **this mooring** of the past? The centuries are conspirators **returning in my dreams despite the years since the divorce** against the sanity and **whatever** majesty **I tire** of the soul. Time and space are but physiological **cones** colors which the eye maketh, but the soul is light; where it is, is day **blazing like July bleakness**; where it was **someone else's babymoon**, is night **with no chance of catching the aurora**; and history is an impertinence and an **unsurvivable** injury if it be any thing more than a cheerful apologue or parable of my being and becoming.

Man is timid and apologetic; he is no longer upright; he dares not say "I think," "I am," but quotes some saint or sage. He is ashamed before the blade of grass or the blowing rose. These roses under my window **look at what you've done** make no reference to former roses **look at it** or to better ones; they are for what they are **hold his eyelids open**; they exist with God today **as do all things, from trilobites to microwaves, which you might as well be** for all He cares. There is no time to them. There is simply the rose inosculation; it is perfect in every moment of its existence but it is never alone. Before a leaf-bud has burst into a storm of ash, its whole life acts in the days we spent reading and singing and eating and talking near him, as close as we could get; in the full-blown flower casting outlines on the snow there is no more memory to be made; in the leafless root there is no less. Its my nature is satisfied and it satisfies nature nature I say again, as if it had a river's course and bend in all moments alike. There is no time to it. But man postpones hastens or remembers; he does not live in the present, but with reverted eye creates anew laments the past, or, heedless of the riches that surround him, hand in the cookie jar, stands on tiptoe to foresee the future. He cannot be happy and strong until he too lives with nature in the present, above time which could not be, for even the apeiron has time, a moment at which it ruptures into order.

This should be plain enough. Yet see what strong intellects dare not yet hear God himself unless he speak the phraseology of I know not what David, or Jeremiah, or Paul, trusting only thoughts I had while crossing the bridge with the breeze at our backs. We shall not always set so great a price on a few texts, on a few lives or will we. We are not like children who repeat by rote the sentences of grandames and tutors as rote learning has largely been phased out, and, as they grow older, of the men of talents and character they chance to see,—painfully recollecting the exact words they spoke I can't imagine anything sillier than psychology; afterwards, except the idea that there is no science of the mind when they come into the point of view which those had who uttered these sayings **how are you holding space for him right now**, they understand them **as a sensible mix of hope and fear** and are willing to let the words go **out of me, as I have too many and they come so cheap**; for at any time they can use words as good when occasion comes. So was it with us, so will it be, if we proceed. If we live truly, we shall see truly. It is as easy for the strong man to be strong, as it is for the weak to be weak. When we have new perception **of the scrapyards as common instead of glorious**, we shall gladly disburthen the memory of its hoarded treasures as old rubbish **and yet we will not believe it; we have seen crushed aluminum glimmer until it blinded us**. When a man lives with God, his voice shall be as sweet as the murmur of the brook and the rustle of the **fields and fields of** corn.

A Barer Sky

What is the worthy form of perception?

The worthy form of perception is final writing. All writing moves toward this end, whether it knows it or not. Yet there are and always will be strains of refusal of finality. In revision, one pens in "more," "not yet," question marks.

The baby is, long before he has form. He inspires quick and sure writing. I know he will close the circle, that seasons will never be what they were before. I hear his father tunelessly singing and sense that song will soon be inaudible from beyond the perimeter of all previous experience.

Events beside the loss of children have inspired sure writing. Evenings after novels. Quiet holidays in empty cities. Raging landscapes, ancestry. Descent. These plaintexts carry no formatting and no typography. No prosody, no line. Gesture and geometry are possibilities in other minds but if they come before the word, they are ornamentation. Writing is signage carved in stone intended to point the way, only as regular as the inexperienced bricklayer's line. Eventually it is time to put away old strategies of composition, including curation, and to write from the string of unfurnished rooms.

The last writing is an immortal child. Terrible in its infancy, it never grows, never sings. It leaves the realm of human contact, or the realm of human contact leaves it. In its liminal state it subsumes mathematics and I begin calling it intuition.

Shorter writings. Crystal passes the threshold for what can be considered alive. Chips of obsidian flake from the wall of the mine. The last writing is born alone under a wedge of moon. But it was abandoned long before that.

Anguish is foreclosure.

*

What passes through the web and falls into the abyss?

On New Year's Eve I forget to wear a real jacket. B and I, freezing, stand on the porch discussing what to do about the abandoned car. Tickets line the windshield like orange confetti. We have reported it at the precinct twice. We have made numerous calls and joined the neighbors in speculating about the woman who left it, young and distressed. The police say that if it is parked illegally, they will come. So we push the car just a few feet into the adjacent no-standing zone, report it again, and leave to join the festivities. When we return in the new year it is gone, like it never happened, someone else's vehicle already parked in its place.

*

We are driving in Staten Island at the end of a late winter morning—B, his cousin, and me. We stop for a heavy breakfast at an Italian restaurant. The cousin's only love at this moment is boxing. He has recently won an important match and must be riding high, though it is hard to tell. After weighing the menu, he says that he will have pasta and compensate by not eating anything the rest of the day. B and I also have pasta. I out-eat even the boxer. He is twenty-four, maybe twenty-five. The two of them would not fit on one side of the booth, so B sits next to me.

We have come to see a stonemason we will shortly learn is closed. We are also hoping to see the turkeys that haunt the Tri-State Area like the dinosaurs they replaced. B asserts that they can fly, that powerlines bow beneath their weight, that they encircle dogwalkers on corners and seek revenge when wronged. One road loops Staten Island like a belt, and when we leave it to go up a hill in search of broken stones and winged predators cutting enormous silhouettes against what's left of snow, someone honks, to remind us where we are.

Returning from the stonemason, we do see a turkey, not a flock, just one, tottering behind a woman in a pink jogging outfit who has also seen it but is not afraid.

*

Pregnant in the backyard of B's parents' house, I am beginning to struggle to cover my new shape. Spring has wetly descended, turning the soil black and bringing out the mosquitoes early.

My son's cousins—the nephews—are four and six years old. The big one thinks the world is apprehensible, while the little one knows that it is not. The younger shares none of the elder's eagerness to sit on a lap and "drive the car" up and down the block. Left behind, I name the trees of the yard to the little one, and when I can't identify, I number the points and say the colors of the leaves.

He and I know there is a snake in this grass. Others doubt; we are in Forest Hills between the stables, parks, and cemeteries; who would believe that walked dogs, backyard mechanics, and landscapers would leave a place for a snake to hide? Why would the rabbits stop to snack so confidently, so vulnerable in the dew? Nonetheless, we are sure. Neither of us have seen it but we are afraid.

The presence of the nephews makes the baby twist in my belly, ready to leap up and play.

*

Spring, warmer than springs before. I am returning from brief abscondment to a more northeasterly state. I am so pregnant it is hard to drive. Someone describes this as my last solo excursion but I find this silly, as I am already not alone.

I narrate the journey stupidly to the baby. A rest stop is a bathroom with a store attached. Motorcycles are beautiful but the people who ride them are not. Music is a way of recalling scents, scents are memories, Emily is a friend from the Midwest relocated, and Mark is only her new partner to us because we do not visit often. Delay, distraction, and detour are permissible when your father's not around, so we pull off at the third beach advertised.

Recently I have been pleading *don't shred Mommy on your way out* and *please be normal despite that glass of wine*, but the beach is no place for begging or prayer or even conversation with the unborn. The beach is for standing a safe distance from the water, nudging the baby with a pushy hand, thinking myself a rather poetic silhouette, swollen in my short brown dress and sore from the weight, observing the simple structures of restrooms and signage, listening to the soft chatter of an older couple as they pass, envisioning a hearty dinner and dismissing it immediately, as there is no room inside me for anything but my son, who I don't know yet is my son—in short, a stopover, a long instant of tans and blues that are only gradients of gray, which is all he knew of life, the only sounds low voices and rushing.

*

Bruised and bleeding, I shuffle from the hospital doors to the parking lot and am grateful to take the elevator, though B's car is parked just one level up. The car is the same as I left it. I am vexed not by the trash on the floor in front of the passenger seat, but by the layer of important documents, which triggers an urge to file so deeply rooted in me that for a moment I forget that our son was born yesterday, and that he is going to die.

I choose the place we go. When we arrive to find it closed, I choose the second place we go. It is almost midnight on Long Island in summer; teenagers emerge from the gas station with slushies and bags of ice and disappear into the darkness; water towers. We are moving at an incredible speed relative to the traffic we are used to.

It takes us only fifteen minutes to travel almost twenty miles. No lights in the houses.

At the diner, the faces of more teenagers, inaudible behind the glass window, select silently from a display of gelato. It is difficult to open my legs far enough to climb out of the car. As I work out how to do it B is concertedly not watching. I shuffle so slowly I get a good look at every car in the lot. By the entrance there is a black pickup, American, 2009 or '10, clean (we are in the suburbs) but not too clean, with the license plate FEAR HIM. Check that out, I say to B, who has also seen it but is not afraid.

*

Where does the soul reside?

Early on one knows what kind of parent one wants to be, at first through medical ethics. The sex of a child is ascertainable just ten weeks after conception because if it is male the mother's blood will read male, or one can request redaction of that information. This is among the happiest qualities an unborn child can impart—not the sex itself, but proof of physical change, chimerism.

"The space of the page is finite," writes Drucker, but the page is not the field of writing. Typesetters say that typesetting is ten percent type and ninety percent space. "The advantage is to 'place' the thing, instead of it wallowing around sort of outside, in the universe," Olson writes of the soul. The thing must be placed if it is to be shared. Set type reiterates centuries of orthodoxy even when it is broken and masterfully or experimentally remade, so too the soul and all it is capable of thinking.

But the child was not meant to be shared or embodied. When they say his liver or his kidneys, I brush it off in disbelief. Some writing never departs from the margins. The worthy form of perception is his warmth against my breast and the cardinals people begin to notice when someone dear to them has died.

*

When my son and I leave our home on the journey toward his grave, home, this "uncommon place," undergoes no physical or spiritual change. There is no question of returning to the house where I grew up, though it is just an hour's drive away from where we bury him on a Monday morning. "At bottom I have already undergone the test of my own view of life," Nietzsche, age thirty-five, writes to his friend Peter Gast of his migraines. "I shall not come to you myself... there are states in which it seems to me more fitting to return to the neighborhood of one's mother, one's home, and the memories of one's childhood." After the funeral, my sister, two friends, and I flee the city up Route 1 into the gnarled wrist of Massachusetts. We could be mistaken for any sedan of New York women on vacation. The muscles I call on to stand me up and sit me down regain their power, and within a few days, all the aches and pains of pregnancy go away.

It is the weekend of the Fourth of July and the weather is drizzly. The colors of sand and sky are the same. The house we have chosen could be called yellow on any other occasion. The four of us move through shopping at the town store, cooking seafood, washing dishes, driving, buying booze, rising early, all in seamless revolutions. I had planned to bring the baby on this same trip later in the summer but had made no real arrangements for it. I had not truly believed that it would happen, that we would put the baby in his oversized hat—and indeed, in his short life, he is only ever outside for a few moments.

When I return without him, home is the same as it always was.

The first half of the year—my pregnancy—is dominated by rain. After the summer an historical drought, then winter begins in earnest. Texts I once found complex and gorgeous drain to their skeletons and then to their rivers, repetitions and spaces between words and grafs. In typesetting, orphans are lines marooned at the bottom of a page, while widows are alone at the top. A cruder way to remember is that orphans have no past and widows, no future—and the cruder way is always more memorable. "Have I made it clear what kind of task I proposed myself in this book? ... It certainly is too bad that I had to obscure and spoil Dionysiac hints with formulas borrowed from Schopenhauer, but there is another feature [which] seems even worse in retrospect... my urge to hope when there was nothing left to hope for." Nietzsche, who had no children, revises his first book with the advantage of hindsight. He prays that God's absolute truth is something else. Traversing the mind of another requires the memorization of constellations which are mnemonics for stars, but if all maps are partial, so is navigation.

*

How does one know it is a universe of chance? Isn't everything we marvel at equal proof of a universe of design? For a shining moment this last question seems thrilling and important, and just as soon it becomes clear that there is hardly any difference.

The news makes its way to me that the rules of baseball are changing again. Pitch clocks, bigger bases, pickoffs, infield shifts, each team starts with a runner on second base after the tenth inning. Constraint writing. Minute changes have unintended effects. The days fill like a scorecard, coded notations in pencil. Sometimes I am up to bat, then I am in the field. The Mets are eliminated and then the Yankees. The voice of the crowd rises feverishly, people in the bars holler at the televisions and pound their fists, but I can only dimly hear them from deep in the outfield where cicadas are screaming.

In school I encounter the notion that writing is an imposition on the mind's prelinguistic sensory and emotional capabilities. I read that this has been studied and can be seen glowing on magnetic images and in child psychology, something "behind" writing that is capable of purer subjectivity, something that experiences more fully and expresses itself in speech, music, and movement, something writing tries and fails to access and convey. Writing is associated with logic, law, power, and depersonalization, and the implications are grim. The usefulness of writing is not questioned, but I sense a desire for a more flexible mode. Had I been my mother perhaps I would have danced my lost child. What would history be in puppetry, mime, programming language, or batik? What would he sound like in theremin; what would he look like in flower? Had he lived, perhaps I would have known. But in writing he becomes more like he was. The feigned distance, the disappearance of anything that looks too much like us into letterfit and ligature, suits him. He becomes not his first name and not our surname, which he never knew, not his parentage nor his circumstance, not even his sleep and what came after. On the page he is each of his potential selves lived to fullness and struck down.

Infield shifts. I stare at the word "bed" and remember the precise moment I stopped recognizing the word from memory in its bedlike shape and was able to hear with my eyes the sounds the letters made. Which one of those understandings was "reading"? Before I understood phonics, was "bed" a different thing? No, it was what it is now: the place where I am shown possibilities before waking into a world less strange, but darker.

*

When does language become more than the word?
Before the baby, I spend the summers at a park that lies at the intersection of two main streets which, despite this, tends toward invisibility. Almost every day these summers, B plays pickup basketball, I read, and then we get drunk with the handful of men who have become friends over the years. I love the park because it is not a scenic place. You may have been there yourself and never known. The summer before the autumn I fall pregnant, all July and into August, I lie on the bench with my purse as a pillow reading Susan Howe's *The Birthmark: Unsettling the Wilderness in American Literary*

History. "A poem can prevent onrushing light going out. Narrow path in the teeth of proof. Fire of words will try us. Grace given to few. Coming home through bent and bias for the sake of why so. Awkward as I am. Here and there invincible things as they are."

The following spring, heavily pregnant, I drive past the park a few times after work, the same purple pair of B's old sneakers swinging from the lamp post as they always have. It is not much as far as fields of dreams go, I apologize to my belly. It is technically within the five boroughs but outside what most people consider New York. The rushing sound is the highway, not the ocean; homeless people sleep here. Here and there invincible things as they are.

From Howe I learn that around the time of the Antinomian Crisis—October 1636 to March 1638—Puritan anxiety about salvation reaches such a level that a New England woman throws her infant into a well so that she can be sure that she is damned. Anne Hutchinson, around whom the Crisis circles, visits Boston women in her "childbirth-travells, wherein shee was not onely skilfull, but readily fell into good discourse with the women about their spiritual estates." I begin to understand that the law of the land is that no law is binding, especially on the birthing mother, the first defector. In this series of images, I do not yet see myself.

When the time comes, I choose for my son the cemetery between my house and the park. The narrow pathway.

In *The Birth-mark*, the landscape of New England is crisscrossed with footprints: religious crisis and the scapegoating of women, colonialism and captivity, textual history and public declaration. Savagery and restoration. All of this in the circle of light in the snow cast by a fire. Sojourns outside, forced or elected, can only be understood within this circle, for there is no proof of elsewhere unless someone returns. Before Jackie, it is still possible to avoid negotiating with the concept of the wilderness altogether.

Then my son slips out. He scrambles away from me and does not return. I see him "transformed—assimilated" as I approach the limit of feeling and am pulled back by the living.

*

But who is He?

A neighbor assures me that all babies go to heaven if they are baptized, then asks, was he? Because my father is nominally Jewish and my mother is miscellaneously spiritual, and because the Ottomans conquered parts of Europe in the violent Middle Ages, my son swims in gray waters eternally or until something, depending how you subscribe. Of this I cannot bring myself to be afraid. Though I wake hot mornings screaming to know where he is, I know where he is, for I decide where he will go when he is still alive, while we are still at the hospital, when we have just been told he will not return home, which I whisper in his ear that I do not believe. O the mothers who don't know where their children are buried, or if they are. My own mother is concerned with laying him to rest in the shade of a tree.

I care less about the shade and more about the view, Manhattan hazy in the west, spitting distance from the narrow road I weave on my way to Costco and B on his way to basketball, the most recent neighbor a beloved grandfather with a smooth, dark stone. A hill so full of beloveds, the gravedigger informs us, the only room they have left is for children's small plots. A niche in the world the perfect size for my boy. Come winter, someone tells me, the skyline will be even sharper in the absence of leaves.

What is winter when it is July forever? Taking a friend from out of state up to the cemetery, the clock inching dangerously close to four thirty when the gates close, it seems as though we will not be able to visit him, though she has come all this way. I drive poorly. Though we are not far from my house, I am lost among the one-ways. Maybe we should call and ask them to stay open, the friend offers, maybe you should let me give you directions, but none of this is necessary, for when the gatekeeper sees my face she truly sees it and is terribly afraid.

*

Another, more distant cousin of B's asks me how old I think he is. I admit that he is tall for thirteen. In the rearview mirror, his forehead and brow are similar to B's, the boxer's, the nephews', and my son's. Angled down, as always, at his phone. This is the boy's first summer on the job, helping his cousins and uncles gut an apartment. At first there was excitement in freedom, in cash, then the realization that work is hard, must be done attentively, and never ends, only pauses. Eighth grade comes before joy in work. He drinks the iced tea I brought him in quick, deep gulps.

B has run out of patience with the boy. You don't 'get' money, you earn it, he says. The boy is not listening. When we drop him off, he thanks me for the ride and the tea, what a polite boy, I say to B. He doesn't listen, B complains. At this I can't help but laugh.

*

Where do we find consolation?

"Labor teaches you how to be a parent," I read sometime in the winter. "Take your breaks."

Between crying jags, I and everyone dear to me smoke a staggering number of cigarettes. All of us had been at the end of our smoking careers. Besides my sister, I met everyone I love by smoking, and in the face of tragedy, everyone I love returns in their true form. We take smoke breaks from holding and admiring him and holding each other in the parking lot of the hospital, then scrub our hands. When we bury him, the men fill his grave, and then B and I smoke after everyone leaves. The ashtray on the back porch, empty for months, overflows, is emptied, overflows, is emptied. I catch sight of B's mother smoking on the corner and cross the street. I wind up with packs of the wrong brands, unfamiliar colors in my purse and recycling. I am offered long cigarettes and needle-thin ones, pouches of nicotine salt for tucking in my lip, vapes in an array of hues and intensities.

To escape town, first I go to the beach. To escape the beach I return to work. To avoid work I go to the bar. To avoiding being at the bar too much, I go to another bar. To escape concern, I arrange numerous social situations and dive into them headfirst. To avoid drowning I stay away from water. Staying away from water, sitting on a stone wall marked private, smoking, I avoid looking at children, especially infants. Trying to figure out how not to be morose around children, I look up infant loss on the internet. To avoid reading the repeat loss forum, I open the blank document, which has always been there for me. To escape the eyes of those who have always been there for me, I make shapes in the blank document, crowding its pure white landscape. Its blankness bears no resemblance to the baby, whose face, if I can say this, was a bit overdetermined, his features already so serious, bright and structured as a church with no shadows. The document as it slowly grows is terrifying in its carcinogenic lack of constraints.

B texts to say he has arrived. I get back in the car. Today it is just the two of us and I don't ask where we're going.

Three White Foxes on the Minaret of the Local Mosque

BEFORE

three white foxes on the minaret of the local mosque
words of discouragement of birds on the minaret

as the bolide notches the tower wireless emits
invisibly from, as memory concatenates, as you

were fought from cold land, as the tempered steel
city of origin is revealed to be an annex that can rip,

as the waning halfmoon and green slats of an instant
stretched over years disappear, as for the first time

while I am looking at gray weeds you turn
birds whisper that it is impossible, I fruitless,

father forgone, February snow shear forgone,
but you do not care, you are turning

AFTER

three white foxes on the minaret of the local mosque
as it is established that you are no one god's son

I refuse to share you with His Representatives
your movement encircled by Attendants

whose holiness in ritual in the face of horror
takes the shape of a plastic comb, your father,

your aunts, concerned with how you will look
when you are Presented, each take your head

I see the rooftops where you were imagined
slant away from weather, a gentle change in which

(Michael tells me) is the only thing you felt
the air around you roomless and still as water

three white foxes on the minaret of the local mosque
ghost movement in the womb eleven days after

weeping against the stone of seventeen-month-old
Julie, died 1877, against the current

that would beach them were sea lions
made of anything except sheer black muscle

against your father who believes there is no other
than suffering, I defend your joy senselessly

I enter a tunnel which occludes time curiously
as radio disappears in the Holland

through which the three of us pass
a shared dream of gray static and fog

three white foxes on the minaret of the local mosque
I had not known they weren't my dreams

though I had read of oneiric transplantation
trickled through French from standard Albanian

the world the way it appears in a mystery novel
hooded figures shiftless in the gorge

punctuated by random violence
always morning in the diner booth

where your father orders an espresso
on the second day of your life, into which I peer

but the surface does not refract, as in your dreams
there is not yet a reflection in the mirror

three white foxes on the minaret of the local mosque
"I am the center / Of a circle of pain / Exceeding

its boundaries in every direction," writes Loy
whose Oda dies a year later of meningitis

"Who was Mary Shelley?" asks Niedecker
who is in the hot air balloon as it rises

who is at the beach watching the tide
who held my shoulders as I writhed

who made you, and why? you were
to fly without me at the age of twelve

for the first time, I was to wave to you
from behind a breachable security line

three white foxes on the minaret of the local mosque
"I am the center / Of a circle of pain / Exceeding

three white foxes on the minaret of the local mosque
ecstatic with pain, I begin to understand the house

as it would have been, look at pictures of nurseries
in disarray after arrival, what is used and unused

what is touched and not believed and sung
in languages that blur around my child

everyone's last guess and best hope, scripts
older than common knowledge, as rain

in its lovely varietals engenders powerful
hydrangeas to be judged by panels, soil ceases

to emanate its enlivening smell, and I grant
everyone permission to lock you away

three white foxes on the minaret of the local mosque
beyond the border, you and I exist together

in the world, we are a memory so difficult
the witnesses cannot testify; I attach a sticker

to my car that says I am allowed here,
this pond, this lot, and so become any other

summer visitor to your vacation town
I meet you in the eyes of year-round dwellers

who ride out black winters and seek not permission
for the night fires they build along the coast

rocked like the loosely anchored shellfish boat
you slip between the gaps between night fires

three white foxes on the minaret of the local mosque
I wake to my sisters huddled at the edge of bed

or on the floor beside my couch in medicated
dreaming, no one wanting to sleep alone

besides the son, who woke only briefly
besides the father, who rarely sleeps

in the dewy hours before the time of living
I become our grandmothers sweatshirted

walking the dogs at dawn, athletic blades
against no fewer than ten children who died

between the old country and this one
cutting away through the cattail marsh

three white foxes on the minaret of the local mosque
what you felt or did not is beyond reason

many envy the likelihood that for you no pain
registered, you never showed distress, your heart

never raced in fear, you never cried, never missed me,
never knew when you were left in the care of others,

never paid taxes, never ate seitan, never experienced
indigestion, humiliation, incarceration, or thirst

many say you were spared in the weeks after
not knowing that I warned you of suffering

that I swore to bring you through it
but you did not listen and would not sign

three white foxes on the minaret of the local mosque
as I watch you reach the edge I cannot cross

weeping ceases in the room as without
the machine you live ten silent minutes

I have already told you everything I know
have told you I love you as many times

as there is time for, as your father, my sisters,
the beloveds disappear, you do not appear

to change but do grow lighter
as the broken circle of my cervix closes

as around your body the pealing restarts
this time unencumbered, as you cannot hear it

V.

I Am Not All Men,
But Something Less and More

And now at last I rise to declare the highest truth: on this subject everything else that remains unsaid is for me to treasure, keep safe, and suffer from; probably cannot be said ascending like straphangers when the train is canceled; for all that we say is the far off remembering of the intuition tunnels. That thought, of what lies beneath, what fearsome material travels there, by what I can now nearest approach to say it, is this enriched uranium. When good is near you, when you have life in yourself,—it is not by any known or appointed way which once brought comfort because the conspiracy lay reassuringly with others; you shall not discern the footprints of any other in pursuit of the culprit; you shall not see the face of man; you shall not hear any name;—the way to understand what happened, the thought of how else, the good of life of joy and sex and wit and merriment, shall be wholly strange and new and moreover tinged with the smell of disinfectant. It shall exclude all other being. You take the way from man, not to man. All persons that ever existed are its fugitive ministers. There shall be no fear in it. Fear and hope are alike beneath it. It asks nothing. There is somewhat low even in hope. We are then in vision. There is nothing that can be called gratitude, nor properly joy. The soul is raised over passion. It seeth identity and eternal causation. It is a perceiving that Truth and Right are. Hence it becomes a Tranquillity out of the knowing that all things go well. **Yours til death, Judah.** Vast spaces of nature **spread-eagle before me**; the Atlantic Ocean, the South Sea; vast intervals of time, years, centuries, are of no account **yet I feel Pangaea splitting in my bones**. This which I think and feel, **the gradual motion of landscape,** underlay that former state of life and circumstances, as it does underlie my present and will always all circumstances, and what is called life and what is called death **and the translucency between.**

Life only avails, not the having lived. **On Monday we will focus on the perfect tense.** Power ceases in the instant of repose; it resides in the moment of transition **at this point you may become violently nauseous and even vomit** from a past to a new state **motherhood**, in the shooting of the gulf, in the darting to an aim, **in the recoil which nudged the protective cuff from my right ear, never to hear properly again.** This one fact the world hates, that the soul becomes, **that the human body can continue living after torture and gunfire and dismemberment and disemboweling;** for that forever degrades the past; turns all riches to poverty, all reputation to a shame; confounds the saint with the rogue; shoves Jesus and Judas equally aside, **life does not truly begin until this moment.** Why then do we prate of self-reliance **when it is clear that in reality there is no other choice?** Inasmuch as the soul is present there will be power not confident but agent **Smith, Satan.** To talk of reliance is a poor external way of speaking. Speak rather of that which relies because it works and is. Who has more soul **dimorphic than I masters me lumpy and feminine**, though he should not raise his finger. **Regardless,** round him **or her** I must revolve by the gravitation of spirits **as in just a few weeks my daughter will start knocking on the door.** Who has less I rule with like facility. **Or is it a boy again?** We fancy it rhetoric when we speak of eminent virtue **blabbering like the adult voices from the cartoon.** We do not yet see that virtue is Height, and that a man or a company of men, plastic and permeable to principles, by the law of nature must overpower and ride all cities, nations, kings, rich men, poets, who are not.

This is the ultimate fact which we so quickly reach on this, as on every topic, the resolution of all into the ever-blessed ONE. Virtue is the governor, the creator, the reality. **It's in your best interest to offer oral sex once a week.** All things real are so by so much virtue as they contain. Hardship, husbandry, hunting, whaling, war, eloquence, personal weight, are somewhat **of a delay from the antinomian perspective,** and engage my respect as examples of the soul's presence and impure action. I see the same law working in nature for conservation and growth. **Peach trees, cicadas, tomatoes heavy on the vine.** The poise of a planet, the bended tree recovering itself from the strong wind, the vital resources of every animal and vegetable, are also demonstrations of the self-sufficing and therefore self-relying soul. **Take the interstate.** All history, from its highest to its trivial passages, is the various record of this power, **dusky semaphores even more majestic when they rise from ruins.**

Thus all concentrates **on a lunch we had at an expensive seafood restaurant, before a trip to the gift shop;** let us not rove; let us sit at home with the cause. Let us stun and astonish the intruding rabble of men and books and institutions by a simple declaration of the divine fact. Bid them take the shoes from off their feet, **throw the female crabs back,** for God is here within, **always auditing.** Let our simplicity judge them, and our docility to our own law **sleepyhead** demonstrate the poverty of nature and fortune beside our native riches.

But now we are a mob **the city is too ready for.** Man does not stand in awe of man, nor is the soul admonished to stay at home, to put itself in communication with the internal ocean, but it goes abroad to beg a cup of water of the urns of men **and once the toothpaste is out of the tube, there has never been a successful return to communal ownership.** We must go alone. Isolation must precede true society **which precedes and follows everything.** I like the silent church **day of catacombs** before the service begins, better than any preaching **traipsing down the ancient Roman road.** How far off, how cool **in your sunglasses,** how chaste the persons look, begirt each one with a precinct or sanctuary. So let us always sit **on the stoop and allow mosquitoes to prickle us.** Why should we assume the faults of our friend, or wife, or father, or child, because they sit around our hearth, or are said to have the same blood? **I am amazed to find myself amazed by an iridescent sunshower.** All men have my blood and I have all men's. **I am not all men, but something less and more.** Not for that will I adopt their petulance or folly, even to the extent of being ashamed of it. But your isolation must not be mechanical **octopus,** but spiritual, that is, must be elevation **or must sink back below, from whence it cannot return.**

At times the whole world seems to be in conspiracy to importune you with emphatic trifles. Friend, client, child, sickness, fear, want, charity, all knock at once at thy closet door and say, "Come out unto us."—Do not spill thy soul; **do not confuse mutual orgasm with mutual feeling;** do not all descend; keep thy state; stay at home **office** in thine own heaven **ensconced;** come not for a moment into their facts, into their hubbub of conflicting appearances, but let in the light of thy law **sure and serene** on their confusion. The power men possess to annoy me I give them by a weak curiosity. No man can come near me but through my act **let one past the goalie.** "What we love that we have, but by desire we bereave ourselves of the love."

If we cannot at once rise to the sanctities of obedience and faith, **the rows of carrels prim and silent,** let us at least resist our temptations, let us enter into the state of war and wake Thor and Woden, courage and constancy, **road slicked with snow** in our Saxon breasts. This is to be done in our smooth times by speaking the truth, **by reaffirming our values when it is clearest no one is listening.** Check this lying hospitality and lying affection. Live no longer to the expectation of these deceived and deceiving people with whom we converse. Say to them, O father, O mother, O wife, O brother, O friend, I have **barely** lived with you after appearances hitherto **but I'd like more credit for trying.** Henceforward I am the truth's. **What is the marker for this moment, the linchpin between two lives?** Be it known unto you that henceforward I obey no law less than the eternal law. I will have no covenants but proximities **and this limp handful of loyalties means little now.** I shall endeavor to nourish my parents, to support my family, to be the chaste husband of one wife,—but these relations I must fill after a new and unprecedented way. I appeal from your customs. I must be myself **multiplied and divided.** I cannot break myself any longer for you, or you, **I say, but of course it is untrue; there is more to be broken all the way down to the atomic level.** If you can love me for what I am, we shall be happier. If you cannot, I will still seek to deserve that you should. I must be myself. I will not hide my tastes or aversions. I will so trust that what is deep **what flows beneath the creek** is holy, that I will do strongly before the sun and moon whatever inly rejoices me and the heart appoints. If you are noble, I will love you; if you are not, I will not hurt you and myself by hypocritical attentions **torque and flounder.** If you are true, but not in the same truth with me, cleave to your companions; I will seek my own **telling of the story of Isaac.** I do this not selfishly but humbly and truly. It is alike your interest, and mine, and all men's, however long we have dwelt in lies, to live in truth, **to wonder why they do not speak on their way up the mountain.** Does this sound harsh today? You will soon love what is dictated by your nature as well as mine, **little seed,** and if we follow the truth it will bring us out safe at last, **safer at least, free of panic and hysteria.**—But so may you give these friends pain. Yes, but I cannot sell my liberty and my power, to save their sensibility. Besides, all persons have their moments of reason, when they look out into the region of absolute truth **as lightning strikes and as quickly vanishes;** then will they justify me and do the same thing.

The populace think that your rejection of popular standards is a rejection of all standard, and mere **mystical** antinomianism; and the bold sensualist **moving against me in the lamplight** will use the name of philosophy to gild his crimes. But the law of consciousness abides **no matter what you take to put yourself to sleep**. There are two confessionals, in one or the other of which we must be shriven **enshrined**. You may fulfil your round of duties by clearing yourself in the direct, or in the reflex way. Consider whether you have satisfied your relations to father, mother, cousin, neighbor, town, cat and dog; whether any of these can upbraid you. But I may also neglect this reflex standard and absolve me to myself. I have my own stern claims and perfect circle. It denies the name of duty to many offices that are called duties. **Check this box if you are self-employed.** But if I can discharge its debts it enables me to dispense with the popular code. If any one imagines that this law is lax, let him keep its commandment one day.

And truly it demands something godlike in him who has cast off the common motives of humanity and has ventured to trust himself for a taskmaster. **Nonsense: Emerson's man does nothing for a soul but he**. High be his heart, faithful his will, clear his sight, that he may in good earnest be doctrine, society, law, to himself, that a simple purpose may be to him as strong as iron necessity is to others. **But what would the simple purpose be, given life and breath? To continue against all odds? To propagate? To insure? To cut down the forest?**

If any man consider the present aspects of what is called by distinction society, he will see the need of these ethics, The sinew and heart of man seem to be drawn out washed out in the laundry and hung palely on the line to dry, and we are become timorous desponding whimperers. We are afraid of truth, afraid of fortune, afraid of death, and afraid of each other, **and afraid of pain most of all**. Our age yields no great and perfect persons. We want men and women who shall renovate life and our social state, but we see that most natures are insolvent; cannot satisfy their own wants, have an ambition out of all proportion to their practical force, and so do lean and beg day and night **the lonely stoner** continually **frees his mind at night**. Our housekeeping is mendicant, our arts, our occupations, our marriages, our religion we have not chosen, but society has chosen for us. We are parlor soldiers, **children playing house**. The rugged battle of fate, where strength is born, we shun.

If our young men miscarry in their first enterprises they lose all heart. If the young merchant fails, men say he is ruined. If the finest genius studies at one of our colleges, and is not installed in an office within one year afterwards, in the cities or suburbs of Boston or New York, it seems to his friends and to himself that he is right in being disheartened and in complaining the rest of his life **though now we have built in a little more time, knowing what we know about the prefrontal cortex**. A sturdy lad from New Hampshire or Vermont **which once lay under three miles of ice**, who in turn tries all the professions, who teams it, farms it, peddles, keeps a school, preaches, edits a newspaper, goes to Congress, buys a township, and so forth, in successive years, and always like a cat falls on his feet, is worth a hundred of these city dolls. He walks abreast with his days and feels no shame in not "studying a profession," for he does not postpone his life, but lives already.

He has not one chance, but a hundred chances. Let a stoic arise who shall reveal the resources of man and tell men they are not leaning willows **crying their fronds into the country road**, but can and must detach themselves; that with the exercise of self-trust, new powers shall appear; **that where Spanish moss grows we do not belong;** that a man is the word made flesh, **steel,** born to shed healing to the nations, **that some of us need help and some won't accept it,** that he should be ashamed of our compassion, **of our desire,** and that the moment he acts from himself, tossing the laws, the books, idolatries and customs out of the window, **he gains no power nor freedom**—we pity him no more but thank and revere him; **but a slim chance** and that teacher shall restore the life of man to splendor and make his name dear to all History.

It is easy to see that a greater self-reliance—a new respect for the divinity in man—must work a revolution in all the offices and relations of men; in their religion; in their education; in their pursuits; their modes of living; their association; in their property; in their speculative views. **The risks are enormous: a lodestar can only be observed from a measured distance; you must walk both within and beside yourself.**

KNOTS

The Sanskrit word for knot ... eventually took on
the meaning of 'book.' *Grantha*. This is because
of the manuscripts. The birch-bark and palm-leaf
manuscripts were bound by a cord drawn through two
holes and knotted.

Don DeLillo

Staples
no wash no dry no carpet
have you seen this man
hotel immaculate dialysis
construction site
nautical bar
windowless Indian restaurant
cakes by Caroline and Andi
neoclassical demo facade
American self-storage
best mechanic

became snitch
seer maniacal forgets
colossal decadence mafia
arcane dandelion sickbay
instantaneous inwards wilder
air but canal
contour scientist
humility locates maladies
have you seen this man
orphan secondary town
pastels

harsh garden
before the fog

waiting for breakfast
all tilts

but does not depend
upon the eyeglass

screwdriver
it's your time

the clear hour
tight and held

arranged shh
in the mind

dream untied
Nachträglichkeit
disjunctive island
ensuing mystery of scheme
and broken dealership
diner counter television
speaking suspect of listeners

cassette knifing purposeless
love nutrition residence
shirked repel abandon
ecosystem hymen refusing
divas inclined just
the cracking hilt
muted rained

then it straightens into a city of rectilinear avenues and
    prides itself
on its considerable insight and clearheadedness

imagine as you breathe that you are the projectile
launched through the target, that you could cleave

blood and rage from speed and accuracy
as if hunting yesterday's self

but no shot
both not us

beloved faces
vanish
quickly as the hated
but where do they
never mind
they all go the same place

collage shame telepathy
driven men
debt where youth
hatched tequila sky
his van
bleeds cave of

the sky burns
with the same chemicals
as the ooze in the port
for which you feel neither
responsible nor absolved
but the third feeling which
both the guilty and innocent
call "implicated," and
though you cannot see them
you know that the roof
of the clouds and the floor
of the canal
are lined with cast-off
evidence, like your soul
never clear water
but a neater scrawl

light in the courtyard
yields softly
as love to work
when night is done

thin heeding snow
overtook laws
slyly foisted
rough latched trinity

rust road
you can only look

harsh rivulets
white bike garlanded

work in your ear
a half seashell

life under anthill moon
narrow motion

for the sake of motion
hoof knife stateroom

there were brothers on the hill
sure as goats and clouds
eels in the national river
mounting sureness in the bread

tears in the water
beatings ensured nourishment
catatonia inherent patrols
dynamite in the national river

the darkness that falls
over the backyard in Michigan
is said to be so complete
no citydweller could fathom
its quick vein, though in daylight
they inner tube and at night
wine flows

if owl sewn
bathing entity underneath
she asks, what is the point
if it is meaningless
but the creek has an end,
a root, submerged
so completely you cannot see it

for Emily

along the underpass ride teens
just as soon they aim
true hit, the smoothie splatters
the joy of mutiny
does not remain
just as soon the gunman
slopes threadbare behind them
overcome with untidy need
and sureness of pursuit

symmetry except what your hands touch
try to mold or build, their barren spaghetti
poorly estimates cost per careful foot and wire
arcing against closed eyes still burns them

so went up the first house and the second fare
takes you only as far as the cemetery
streets of rubber, labor, strippers, ceremony
the destroyed tune a lonesome rhythm

WHAT WILL THE THIRD SHAPE BE

what will the third shape be
as April resolves in the extra room
as fiberglass sags and resolution grows
as bodies that once sought heat
are electrically repulsed

the swaying of the pendulum
the movement of the vine

like enclosure of farmland
the physics of walls is doubt
the load-bearing gamble hits
by continuing to stand, stress
upon the keystone, the first shape
never becomes immeasurable
the second shape, shoulders back
in victory, celebrates itself, the post,
streetlamp, and the swish
blames the wind for misdirection
the third shape is not like its parents
having no knowledge and no economy
as the blur in which it grows
grows too, where no auditory
structures have been formed as yet
and so it cannot disobey

as delay is the only humane action
as extending possibility into the future
is one form of love, and shadow
is the other

profitably immense, sun
asks that the bridge be raised
shoulder high in the lot

a water-damaged television
skyline, which in your lifetime
I pray will hardly transform

always there will be signs
of refusal of opacity

lossy compression
then two more nights

biting down on the comb
surviving by counterpressure

pain endurable because it is
productive, though also

subtractive, etching in relief
time's swath unknown

in the other room, a foreign landscape
midwives interpret descent's

keen song, read progression
from screaming's tenor, between

black clock's stutter and the sleep
of the father, even at its thickest

only the topmost layer, water
from which there is no recovery

the nightly challenge is to emerge
to die into the dream of the glass field
of crawling, not to back away from the

fence, for obtaining a visa elsewhere
is impossible and the lie must hold
that each is the final mile

as land becomes only words
the alternative is born and rises
we see it at the edges, in faces

into its perfect ear I hush my question
but die into morning long before
the shape apprehends language

do not pursue burrowing owls
reads the sign on the landfill-
sanctuary, but birdwatchers
will not be cowed, shining light
over modest hills of homes

into what do owls burrow,
which substrate of humming-
bird and public sculpture-
scented earth, hazy bay
where Allison and I sit down

not to discuss that I still think I
can speak with you, soil owl,
but to enunciate the unearthly
cost of living in the living world

VI.

To Live and Sing Alone

In what prayers do men allow themselves! That which they call a holy office is not so much as brave and manly. Prayer looks abroad **musty churches and poorly painted saints** and asks for some foreign addition to come through some foreign virtue, and loses itself in endless mazes of natural and supernatural, and mediatorial and miraculous, **questions I postpone when we're together.** Prayer that craves a particular commodity, any thing less than all good, is vicious, **arm across my belly squeezing tight.** Prayer is the contemplation of the facts of life **of what one allows to enter the body** from the highest point of view. It is the soliloquy of a beholding and jubilant soul. It is the spirit of God pronouncing his works good. But prayer as a means to effect a private end is meanness and theft. It supposes dualism and not unity in nature and consciousness. **There is dualism, though, is there not, there is lack; there is filling it.** As soon as the man is at one with God, he will not beg. He will then see prayer in all action. The prayer of the farmer kneeling in his field to weed it **composing / antagonist**, the prayer of the rower kneeling with the stroke of his oar, are true prayers heard throughout nature, though for cheap ends **don't stop, right there, don't stop.** Caratach, in Fletcher's Bonduca, when admonished to inquire the mind of the god Audate, replies, "His hidden meaning lies in our endeavors; Our valors are our best gods." **He chose; you had nothing to do with it.**

Another sort of false prayers are our regrets. Discontent is the want of self-reliance: it is infirmity of will. Regret calamities if you can thereby help the sufferer; if not, attend your own work **the blank page** and already the evil begins to be repaired **replaced with new pleasure**. Our sympathy is just as base **and difficult to muster**. We come to them who weep foolishly and sit down and cry for company, instead of imparting to them truth and health in rough electric shocks, putting them once more in communication with their own reason. The secret of fortune is joy in our hands **the secret**. Welcome evermore to gods and men is the self-helping man **who never quite here, also never leaves**. For him all doors are flung wide; him all tongues greet, all honors crown, all eyes follow with desire. Our love goes out to him and embraces him because he did not need it **us**. We solicitously and apologetically caress and celebrate him because he held on his way **refused to apologize** and scorned our disapprobation. The gods love him because men hated him. "To the persevering mortal," said Zoroaster, "the blessed Immortals are swift."

As men's prayers are a disease of the will, so are their creeds a disease of the intellect. They say with those foolish Israelites, "Let not God speak to us, lest we die. Speak thou, speak any man with us, and we will obey." Everywhere I am hindered of meeting God in my brother, **never just one nor one among others,** because he has shut his own temple doors and recites fables merely of his brother's, or his brother's brother's God. Every new mind is a new classification. If it prove a mind of uncommon activity and power, a Locke, a Lavoisier, a Hutton, a Bentham, a Fourier, **we will never know; this too,** it imposes its classification on other men, and lo! a new system. In proportion to the depth of the thought, and so to the number of the objects it touches and brings within reach of the pupil, is his complacency. **The primacy of the relation between first, second, and third.** But chiefly is this apparent in creeds and churches, which are also classifications of some powerful mind acting on the elemental thought of duty, and man's relation to the Highest. Such is Calvinism, Quakerism, Swedenborgism, **a directness of address, sudden brightness**. The pupil takes the same delight in subordinating every thing to the new terminology as a girl who has just learned botany in seeing a new earth and new seasons thereby. It will happen for a time that the pupil will find his intellectual power has grown by the study of his master's mind. But in all unbalanced minds the classification is idolized **made to fit**, passes for the end and not for a speedily exhaustible means, so that the walls of the system blend to their eye in the remote horizon with the walls of the universe; the luminaries of heaven seem to them hung on the arch their master built. **Are you my master?** They cannot imagine how you aliens have any right to see,—how you can see; 'It must be somehow that you stole the light from us.' They do not yet perceive that light, unsystematic, indomitable, will break into any cabin, even into theirs **through the planks of the house they have carefully laid**. Let them chirp awhile and call it their own, **this plot of time where they take up brief residence**. If they are honest and do well, presently their neat new pinfold will be too straight and low, will crack, will lean, will rot and vanish, and the immortal light, all young and joyful, million-orbed, million-colored, will beam over the universe as on the first morning.

It is for want of self-culture that the superstition of traveling, whose idols are Italy, England, Egypt, retains its fascination for all educated Americans. They who made England, Italy, or Greece venerable in the imagination did so by sticking fast where they were, like an axis of the earth **upon which all tilts but does not depend**. In manly hours we feel that duty is our place **that our forebearers did not clatter down the ancient Roman road**. The soul is no traveler; **he defends us from imagined invaders;** the wise man stays at home, and when his necessities, his duties, on any occasion call him from his house, or into foreign lands, he is at home still **his paranoid landscape** and shall make men sensible by the expression of his countenance **a weapon** that he goes, the missionary of wisdom and virtue, and visits cities and men like a sovereign and not like an interloper or a valet **but what kills us is what grows within**.

I have no churlish objection to the circumnavigation of the globe for the purposes of art, of study, and benevolence, so that the man is first domesticated **housebroken**, or does not go abroad with the hope of finding somewhat greater than he knows. He who travels to be amused, or to get somewhat which he does not carry, travels away from himself, and grows old even in youth among old things. In Thebes, in Palmyra, his will and mind have become old and dilapidated as they, **entropy in reverse**. He carries ruins to ruins. **He would have seen the meadowlands only from the car window, in swift passing.**

Traveling is a fool's paradise. Our first journeys discover to us the indifference of places. At home I dream that at Naples, at Rome, sore and unwieldy but in good spirits, I can be intoxicated with beauty and lose my sadness and feel mostly hunger. I pack my trunk, embrace my friends, embark on the sea and at last wake up in Naples, and there beside me is the stern fact, the sad self, unrelenting, identical, that I fled from, no different adjacent to Vesuvius. I seek the Vatican and the palaces but do not bother to apply for entry. I affect to be intoxicated with sights and suggestions, but I am not intoxicated. My giant goes with me wherever I go and kicks me behind the ribs.

But the rage and fear of traveling is a symptom of a deeper unsoundness affecting the whole intellectual action which I am careful not to write off as dips in the blood sugar. The intellect is vagabond rage and fear and platitudinous contentment alternating swiftly even in the span of a single conversation, and our system of education fosters restlessness no matter how I try to pay attention. Our minds travel when our bodies are forced to stay at home. We imitate normal responses; and what is imitation but the traveling of the mind to a place in the distant past, but even then, I suspect we were the same people? Our houses are built with foreign taste; our shelves are garnished with foreign ornaments; our opinions, our tastes, our faculties, lean, and follow the Past and the Distant, recognizing each other in themselves. The soul created the arts wherever they have flourished, also where they have suffered most. It was in his own mind that the artist sought his model and labored to bring it out of the marble. It was an application of his own thought to the thing to be done and the conditions to be observed. And why need we copy the Doric or the Gothic model **when there is time yet to sculpt a caryatid?** Beauty, convenience, grandeur of thought and quaint expression are as near to us as to any, and if the American artist will study with hope and love the precise thing to be done by him, considering the climate, the soil, the length of the day, the wants of the people, the habit and form of the government, **and the coming end of times,** he will create a house in which all these will find themselves fitted, and taste and sentiment will be satisfied also. **Yet were he to do all this, it would still not be enough. No matter what he builds the rest of his lifetime, you will not be there.**

Insist on yourself; never imitate. Your own grift you can present every moment with the cumulative force of a whole life's cultivation **can get big ideas into punchy little sentences;** but of the adopted talent of another you have only an extemporaneous half possession **couldn't invent the wheel from scratch if you had a thousand years to do it.** That which each can do best, none but his Maker can teach him. **Are you my Maker?** No man yet knows what it is, nor can, till that person has exhibited it. Where is the master who could have taught Shakspeare? **It was the blurst of times.** Where is the master who could have instructed Franklin, or Washington, or Bacon, or Newton? Every great man is a unique. The Scipionism of Scipio is precisely that part he could not borrow **a piece of paper from your neighbor and please, next time, come prepared.** Shakspeare will never be made by the study of Shakspeare. Do that which is assigned you, and you cannot hope too much or dare too much. There is at this moment for you an utterance brave and grand as that of the colossal chisel of Phidias, or trowel of the Egyptians, or the pen of Moses or Dante, but different from all these. Not possibly will the soul, all rich, all eloquent, with thousand-cloven tongue, deign to repeat itself **this is the tragedy**; but if you can hear what these patriarchs say, surely you can reply to them in the same pitch of voice; for the ear and the tongue are two organs of one nature **wordlessness**. Abide in the simple and noble regions of thy life, obey thy heart and thou shalt reproduce the Foreworld **Foreword** again.

As our Religion, our Education, our Art look abroad, so does our spirit of society. All men plume themselves on the improvement of society, and no man improves. **Nothing ever happens.**

Society never advances, **never gives up its oldest rituals, never fails to marvel at its most meager achievements**. It recedes as fast on one side as it gains on the other. Its progress is only apparent like the workers of a treadmill. It undergoes continual changes; it is barbarous, it is civilized, it is christianized, it is rich, it is scientific, **it is saved**; but this change is not amelioration. For every thing that is given something is taken **from the mother, a living organ, in the frenzy of the first moments after birth**. Society acquires new arts and loses old instincts **laughs at the idea that more pain is even possible**. What a contrast between the well-clad, reading, writing, thinking **female** American, with a watch, a pencil and a bill of exchange in his pocket, and the naked New Zealander, whose property is a club, a spear, a mat and an undivided twentieth of a shed to sleep under, **traveling by boat between the fjords**. But compare the health of the two men and you see that his aboriginal strength, the white man has lost. If the traveler tell us truly, strike the savage with a broad axe and in a day or two the flesh shall unite and heal as if you struck the blow into soft pitch, and the same blow shall send the white man to his grave.

The civilized man has built a coach, but has lost the use of his feet. He is supported on crutches, but lacks so much support of muscle. He has got a fine Geneva watch, but he has lost the skill to tell the hour by the sun. A Greenwich nautical almanac he has, and so being sure of the information when he wants it, the man in the street does not know a star in the sky. The solstice he does not observe; the equinox he knows as little, **passing like the long days of an alien planet**; and the whole bright calendar of the year **which can be any length** is without a dial in his mind **though the monthly calendar cannot slip his grasp**. His notebooks impair his memory: his libraries overload his wit; **he orates and orates;** the insurance-office increases the number of accidents; and it may be a question whether machinery does not encumber; whether we have not lost by refinement some energy, by a christianity entrenched in establishments and forms some vigor of wild virtue **that he can neither shed entirely, nor regain, caught between the human and animal**. For every stoic was a stoic; but in Christendom where is the Christian?

There is no more deviation in the moral standard than in the standard of height or bulk. No greater men are now than ever were **one less**. A singular equality may be observed between the great men of the first and of the last ages; nor can all the science, art, religion, and philosophy of the nineteenth century avail to educate greater men than Plutarch's heroes, three or four and twenty centuries ago. Not in time is the race progressive. Phocion, Socrates, Anaxagoras, Diogenes, are great men, but they leave no class. He who is really of their class will not be called by their name, but be wholly his own man, and in his turn the founder of a sect. **What came next was turgid and banal; speeches, tears, nausea at the sentimentality of one's parents; more oration, finitude, appointments, bank checks.** The arts and inventions of each period **September** are only its costume **with its back-to-school smell** and do not invigorate men. The harm of the improved machinery may compensate its good. **The banks of the** Hudson **warm with new life during the pandemic's quiet years** and Behring accomplished so much in their fishing-boats as to astonish Parry and Franklin, whose equipment exhausted the resources of science and art **and dolphins**. Galileo, with an opera-glass, discovered a more splendid series of facts than any one since. Columbus found the New World in an undecked boat. It is curious to see the periodical disuse and perishing of means and machinery which were introduced with loud laudation a few years or centuries before. The great genius returns to essential man **shudders to think what essential woman might be**. We reckoned the improvements of the art of war among the triumphs of science, and yet Napoleon conquered Europe by the Bivouac **crude shelter**, which consisted of falling back on naked valor and disencumbering it of all aids **which as it turns out is not what you want in an emergency**. The Emperor held it impossible to make a perfect army, says Las Cases, "without abolishing our arms, magazines, commissaries and carriages, until, in imitation of the Roman custom, the soldier should receive his supply of corn, grind it in his hand-mill and bake his bread himself."

Society is a **rogue** wave. The wave moves onward, but the water of which it is composed does not. The same particle does not rise from the valley to the ridge. Its unity is only phenomenal **but the phenomena repeat every moment**. The persons who make up a nation today, die, and their experience **does not die** with them. **The valley and the ridge may be constituted of different particles, but no one could deny their participation in one symphonic motion.**

And so **we must try to come to an end here, having yet to discuss** the reliance on Property, including the reliance on governments which protect it, **having noted that it** is the want of self-reliance **also known as dependency which makes things progress, no matter what Emerson says.** Men have looked away from themselves **and this truth** and at things so long that they have come to esteem what they call the soul's progress **a thing that stands on its own legs**, namely, the religious, learned and civil institutions as guards of property, and they deprecate assaults on these, because they feel them to be assaults on property—**they feel they have earned the right to live and sing alone**. They measure their esteem of each other by what each has, and not by what each is. But a cultivated man becomes ashamed of his property, ashamed of what he has, out of new respect for his **integrated** being. Especially he hates what he has if he sees that it is accidental, **yet we know all solid surfaces to be infinitesimally porous—whether it** came to him by inheritance, or gift, or crime, **he cannot return the gift his mother gave him;**

then he feels that it is not having; it does not belong to him, has no root in him, and merely lies there because no revolution or no robber takes it away. **The road where they used to hold the drag races is pocked with speed bumps.** But that which a man is, does always by necessity acquire, and what the man acquires, is permanent **experience** and living property, which does not wait the beck of rulers, or mobs, or revolutions, or fire, or storm, or bankruptcies, but perpetually renews itself wherever the man is put. "Thy lot or portion of life," said the Caliph Ali, "is seeking after thee; therefore be at rest from seeking after if." **It could have gone any other way.** Our dependence on these foreign goods leads us to our slavish respect for numbers **statistics**. The political parties meet in numerous conventions **subway series**; the greater the **grand** concourse and with each new uproar of announcement, The delegation from Essex! The Democrats from New Hampshire! The Whigs of Maine! the young patriot feels himself stronger than before by a new thousand of eyes and arms. **The ferocious beauty of crowds.** In like manner the reformers summon conventions and vote and resolve in multitude. **To be pulled beneath this current would be sweet and loud as any happy union.** But not so O friends! will the God deign to enter **penetrate** and inhabit you, but by a method precisely the reverse. It is only as a man puts off from himself **loses his chains** all external support and stands alone that I see him to be strong and to prevail. He is weaker by every recruit to his banner. Is not a man better than a town? Ask nothing of men, and **they will still disappoint you**, in the endless mutation **of self to self**, thou only firm column must presently appear the upholder of all that surrounds thee **knowing that**

what appears does so only for an instant. He who knows that power is in the soul, that he is weak only because he has looked for good out of him and elsewhere, and, so perceiving, throws himself **into the water** unhesitatingly on his thought, **dives**, instantly rights himself, stands in the erect position, **treading waves that threaten to swallow him,** commands his limbs, works miracles **and just as soon drowns**; just as a man who stands on his feet is stronger than a man who stands on his head.

So use all that is called Fortune. Most men gamble with her, and gain all, and lose all, **everything**, as her wheel rolls. But do thou leave as unlawful **unaccountable** these winnings, and deal with **son's** Cause and **murderous** Effect, the chancellors of God. In the Will **I left you what I had** worked for and acquired, **not knowing** and **not truly understanding that** thou hast chained the wheel of Chance, and shalt always drag her after thee. A political victory, **a strong poem,** a rise of rents, **the discovery of a new and quiet lake in the heat of summer,** the recovery of your sick or the return of your absent friend, or some other quite external event raises your spirits, and you think good days are preparing for you. Do not believe it **which I whispered in your ear that I did not believe.** It can never be so **June again.** Nothing can bring you peace but **finding out for** yourself. Nothing **nothing** can bring you peace but the triumph of principles.

Acknowledgments

Lines and titles are borrowed from: Arakawa & Madeline Gins, blueprints for the Reversible Destiny projects; Samuel Beckett, "All Strange Away"; Charles Bernstein, Bruce Andrews, Ray DiPalma, Steve McCaffery, and Ron Silliman, *LEGEND* (a five-way collaborative text); Charles Bukowski, "Raw with Love"; Don DeLillo, *The Names*; Emily Dickinson, letters; Fyodor Dostoyevsky, *Crime and Punishment* (translation my own with help from M. Judge); Johanna Drucker, *Diagrammatic Writing*; Ralph Waldo Emerson, "On Self-Reliance"; David Hall, *The Antinomian Controversy*; Susan Howe, poems and essays; James Joyce, *A Portrait of the Artist as a Young Man*; Ismail Kadare, *The Palace of Dreams*; Karl Ove Knausgård, *A Time for Everything*; Pierre Klossowski, *Nietzsche and the Vicious Circle*; unpublished titles by Mina Loy via Matt Hofer, *Omnicompetent Modernists: Poetry, Politics, and the Public Sphere*; Mina Loy, "Parturition"; Lorine Niedecker, "Who was Mary Shelley"; Cormac McCarthy, *The Orchard Keeper*; Charles Olson, *Proprioception*; George Oppen, "From a Photograph"; Wallace Stevens, "Anatomy of Monotony"; Rebekah Smith, "Summer in St. Petersberg (or, My Nerves Are Shot)"; and William Carlos Williams, *Spring and All*.

The poems in the section "Knots" were written with the help of an online anagram generator. Each poem contains at least two lines that are anagrams of each other.

Thank you to Beautiful Days Press and Bottlecap Press for allowing me to republish sections of my chapbooks *The Stay Behind* and *Solar Inverter*. Excerpts from this collection appeared in *CutBank, Dialogist, Foundry Journal, Heavy Feather Review, Hobart Pulp, Little Mirror, Pairs, Poetry Northwest, Rampage Party* (with a broadside designed and printed by Margaret Yapp), *Sixth Finch, Tyger Quarterly*, and *Works & Days*.

For their guidance, inspiration, and steadiness, I am grateful to my editors; Allison Henry; Lee Norton; Joan Richardson; Kal Victor; the Sunday reading group; and to my families at home, work, play, and school.

This book is for Alana, Gili, and Sue; for Besnik; for the beansprout; and most of all, for Jackie, wherever I may find you.

SERENA SOLIN lives in Queens, NY. Previous chapbooks include *Solar Inverter* (Bottlecap) and *The Stay Behind* (Beautiful Days Press). Solin's poems and essays have appeared in *CutBank, Denver Quarterly, FENCE, Sixth Finch*, and elsewhere. She is a member of the Ugly Duckling Presse editorial collective and a PhD candidate in the English program at the CUNY Graduate Center.

A Barer Sky
Copyright © Serena Solin, 2026

ISBN 978-1-959708-20-9

First Edition, 2026 — 1,200 copies

Winter Editions, Brooklyn, New York
wintereditions.net

Library of Congress Control Number: 2026932092

Distributed by Asterism Books (US) and Public Knowledge (UK).

Cover image courtesy of Pro Dunk (produnk.com). Typeset in Heldane, a renaissance-inspired serif designed by Kris Sowersby for Klim Type Foundry, and Zirkon, a contemporary gothic designed by Tobias Rechsteiner for Grilli Type. Design based on series templates developed in consultation with Andrew Bourne.

This book was printed and bound in Lithuania by BALTO print with Munken papers. Manufactured by Arctic Paper in Sweden, Munken meets EU Ecolabel, Forest Stewardship Council, and Cradle to Cradle certification standards.

WE is grateful for the support of our subscribers, and extends special thanks to recent Supporting and Lifetime Subscribers: Anonymous (2), Anonymous (in memory of the Beaubiens), Yevgeniy Fiks, and Katy Lederer.

WE is a member of the Community of Literary Magazines and Presses (CLMP) and of Poetry Corp., a publishing cooperative. Tax-deductible donations are much appreciated and should be made through our fiscal sponsor, Ether Sea Projects, Inc.